American National Standard
ASNT Standard Topical Outlines for
Qualification of Nondestructive Testing Personnel

Secretariat

The American Society for Nondestructive Testing, Inc.

Approved June 7, 2011.

American National Standards Institute

Abstract

This standard applies to personnel whose specific tasks or jobs require appropriate knowledge of the technical principles underlying nondestructive testing (NDT) methods for which they have responsibilities within the scope of their employment. These specific tasks or jobs include, but are not limited to, performing, specifying, reviewing, monitoring, supervising, and evaluating NDT work.

To the extent applicable to the standard set forth herein, The American Society for Nondestructive Testing, Inc. (ASNT) does not assume the validity or invalidity, enforceability or unenforceability of patent rights, registered trademarks or copyrights in connection with any item referred to in this standard, study materials, or examinations. Users of this standard, study materials, or examinations are further cautioned and expressly advised that determination of the validity or enforceability of any such patent rights, trademarks, or copyrights, and the risk of the infringement of such rights through misuse of protected materials are the responsibility of the user. Reference to or pictorial depiction of specific types of products or equipment are for purposes of illustration only and do not represent the endorsement of such products or equipment by ASNT.

Employers or other persons utilizing nondestructive testing services are cautioned that they retain full responsibility for ultimate determination of the qualifications of NDT personnel and for the certification process. The process of personnel qualification and certification as detailed in the standard does not relieve the employer of the ultimate legal responsibility to ensure that the NDT personnel are fully qualified for the tasks being undertaken.

This standard is subject to revision or withdrawal at any time by ASNT.

American National Standard

American National Standard Approval of an American National Standard requires verification by ANSI that the requirements for due process, consensus, and other criteria for approval have been met by the standards developer.

Consensus is established when, in the judgment of the ANSI Board of Standards Review, substantial agreement has been reached by directly and materially affected interests. Substantial agreement means much more than a simple majority, but not necessarily unanimity. Consensus requires that all views and objections be considered, and that a concerted effort be made toward their resolution.

The use of American National Standards is completely voluntary; their existence does not in any respect preclude anyone, whether they have approved the standards or not, from manufacturing, marketing, purchasing or using products, processes, or products not conforming to the standards.

The American National Standards Institute does not develop standards and will in no circumstances give an interpretation of any American National Standard. Moreover, no person shall have the right or authority to issue an interpretation of an American National Standard in the name of the American National Standards Institute.

CAUTION NOTICE: This American National Standard may be revised or withdrawn at any time. The procedures of the American National Standards Institute require that action be taken periodically to reaffirm, revise, or withdraw this standard. Purchasers of American National Standards may receive current information on all standards by calling or writing the American National Standards Institute.

first printing 08/11
second printing with corrections 05/12
third printing with corrections 02/13
ebook 06/13
fourth printing 10/13
fifth printing 10/14 with corrections

Errata, if available for this printing, may be obtained from ASNT's web site, www.asnt.org.

ISBN-13: 978-1-57117-221-1 (print)
ISBN-13: 978-1-57117-252-5 (ebook)

Printed in the United States of America.

Published by: The American Society for Nondestructive Testing, Inc.
                1711 Arlingate Lane
                Columbus, OH 43228-0518
                www.asnt.org

Edited by: Cynthia M. Leeman, Educational Materials Supervisor
Assisted by: Bob Conklin, Educational Materials Editor

Tim Jones, Senior Manager of Publications

ASNT Mission Statement:
ASNT exists to create a safer world by promoting the profession and technologies of nondestructive testing.

Foreword

(This foreword is not part of American National Standard CP-105-2011.)

An essential element in the effectiveness of nondestructive testing (NDT) is the qualification of the personnel who are responsible for and who perform nondestructive testing. Formal training is an important and necessary element in acquiring the skills necessary to effectively perform nondestructive tests.

The American Society for Nondestructive Testing, Inc. (ASNT) has, therefore, undertaken the preparation and publication of this standard which specifies the body of knowledge to be used as part of a training program qualifying and certifying NDT personnel.

The ASNT Standard Topical Outlines for Qualification of Nondestructive Testing Personnel (Document No. ASNT-CP-105) was initially processed and approved for submittal to the American National Standards Institute (ANSI) by the ASNT Standards Development Committee. This revision was processed by the ASNT Standards Development Committee. Committee approval of the standard does not necessarily imply that all committee members voted for its approval. At the time it approved this standard, the Standards Development Committee had the following members:

Michael E. McDaniel, SDC Chair
Ronald T. Nisbet, SDC Vice Chair
Matthew L. Patience, CP-105 Chair
Charles Longo, Staff Secretary
George C. Belev
Paul E. Deeds, Jr.
Darrell W. Harris
Victor Hernandez
Thomas L. Payne
William C. Plumstead, Sr.
Michael J. Ruddy
Rick L. Ruhge
Marvin W. Trimm
Michael L. Turnbow
David H. Vaughn
William C. Veal
Sharon I. Vukelich
Margaret (Peg) Whytsell

The outlines contained in this American National Standard were approved by the ASNT Technical and Educational (T&E) Council through its method committees. At the time the standard was approved, the T&E Council, Methods Division had the following members:

CONTENTS

ASNT Standard Topical Outlines for Qualification of Nondestructive Testing Personnel

1.0 Scope

    1.1   This standard establishes the minimum topical outline requirements for the qualification of nondestructive testing (NDT) personnel.

    1.2   This standard details the minimum training course content for NDT personnel.

    1.3   The amount of time spent on each topic in each method should be determined by the NDT Level III and the applicable certification document.

    1.4   These topical outlines are progressive; i.e., consideration as Level I is based on satisfactory completion of the Level I training course; consideration as Level II is based on satisfactory completion of both Level I and Level II training courses.

    1.5   Topics in the outlines may be deleted or expanded to meet the employer's specific applications or for limited certification, unless stated otherwise by the applicable certification procedure or written practice.

Acoustic Emission Testing Level I Topical Outline

Basic Acoustic Emission Physics Course

1.0 Principles of Acoustic Emission Testing
    1.1 Characteristics of acoustic emission
        1.1.1 Continuous emission
        1.1.2 Burst emission
        1.1.3 Emission/signal levels and frequencies
    1.2 Sources of acoustic emission
        1.2.1 Sources in crystalline materials – introduction
        1.2.2 Sources in nonmetals – introduction
        1.2.3 Sources in composites – introduction
        1.2.4 Other sources
    1.3 Wave propagation – introduction
        1.3.1 Wave velocity in materials
        1.3.2 Attenuation
        1.3.3 Reflections, multiple paths
        1.3.4 Source input versus signal output
    1.4 Repeated loadings: Kaiser and Felicity effects and Felicity ratio
        1.4.1 In metals
        1.4.2 In composites
    1.5 Terminology (refer to AE Glossary, ASTM E 1316)

2.0 Sensing the AE Wave
    2.1 Sensors
        2.1.1 Principles of operation
        2.1.2 Construction
        2.1.3 Frequency
    2.2 Sensor attachment
        2.2.1 Coupling materials
        2.2.2 Attachment devices

Basic Acoustic Emission Technique Course

1.0 Instrumentation and Signal Processing
    1.1 Cables
        1.1.1 Coaxial cable
        1.1.2 Twisted pair cable
        1.1.3 Noise problems in cables
        1.1.4 Connectors
    1.2 Signal conditioning
        1.2.1 Preamplifiers
        1.2.2 Amplifiers
        1.2.3 Filters
        1.2.4 Units of gain measurement
    1.3 Signal detection
        1.3.1 Threshold comparator
        1.3.2 Units of threshold measurement
        1.3.3 Sensitivity determined by gain and/or threshold
    1.4 Signal processing
        1.4.1 Waveform characteristics
        1.4.2 Discrimination techniques
        1.4.3 Distribution techniques
    1.5 Source location techniques

        1.5.1   Single channel location
        1.5.2   Linear location
        1.5.3   Planar location
        1.5.4   Other location techniques
   1.6   Acoustic emission test systems
        1.6.1   Single channel systems
        1.6.2   Multi-channel systems
        1.6.3   Dedicated industrial systems
   1.7   Accessory techniques
        1.7.1   Audio indicators
        1.7.2   X-Y and strip chart recording
        1.7.3   Oscilloscopes
        1.7.4   Others

2.0   Acoustic Emission Test Techniques
   2.1   Equipment calibration and setup for test
        2.1.1   Calibration signal generation techniques
        2.1.2   Calibration procedures
        2.1.3   Sensor placement
        2.1.4   Adjustment of equipment controls
        2.1.5   Discrimination technique adjustments
   2.2   Loading procedures
        2.2.1   Type of loading
        2.2.2   Maximum test load
        2.2.3   Load holds
        2.2.4   Repeated and programmed loadings
        2.2.5   Rate of loading
   2.3   Data display
        2.3.1   Selection of display mode
        2.3.2   Use and reading of different kinds of display
   2.4   Noise sources and pre-test identification techniques
        2.4.1   Electromagnetic noise
        2.4.2   Mechanical noise
   2.5   Precautions against noise
        2.5.1   Electrical shielding
        2.5.2   Electronic techniques
        2.5.3   Prevention of movement
        2.5.4   Attenuating materials and applications
   2.6   Data interpretation and evaluation: introduction
        2.6.1   Separating relevant acoustic emission indications from noise
        2.6.2   Accept/reject techniques and evaluation criteria
   2.7   Reports
        2.7.1   Purpose
        2.7.2   Content and structure

3.0   Codes, Standards and Procedures
   3.1   Guide-type standards (glossaries, calibration, etc.)
   3.2   Standardized/codified acoustic emission test procedures
   3.3   User-developed test procedures

4.0   Applications of Acoustic Emission Testing (course should include at least 3 categories from 4.1 and at least 4 categories from 4.2)
   4.1   Laboratory studies (material characterization)
        4.1.1   Crack growth and fracture mechanics
        4.1.2   Environmentally assisted cracking
        4.1.3   Dislocation movement (metals)
        4.1.4   Clarifying deformation mechanisms (composites)
        4.1.5   Phase transformation and phase stability
        4.1.6   Creep

4.1.7   Residual stress
4.1.8   Corrosion
4.1.9   Fatigue
4.1.10 Rupture
4.1.11 Ductile/brittle transition
4.1.12 Other material characterization applications
4.2   Structural applications
4.2.1   Pressure vessels (metal)
4.2.2   Storage tanks (metal)
4.2.3   Pressure vessels/storage tanks (composite)
4.2.4   Piping and pipelines
4.2.5   Bucket trucks
4.2.6   Aircraft
4.2.7   Bridges
4.2.8   Mines
4.2.9   Dams, earthen slopes
4.2.10 Pumps, valves, etc.
4.2.11 Rotating plant
4.2.12 In-process weld monitoring
4.2.13 Leak detection and monitorin
4.2.14 Other structural applications

Acoustic Emission Testing Level II Topical Outline

Acoustic Emission Physics Course

1.0   Principles of Acoustic Emission Testing
    1.1   Characteristics of acoustic emission testing
        1.1.1   Introductory concepts of source, propagation, measurement, display, evaluation
        1.1.2   Relationships between acoustic emission and other NDT methods
        1.1.3   Significance of applied load in acoustic emission testing
        1.1.4   Basic math review (exponents, graphing, metric units)
    1.2   Materials and deformation
        1.2.1   Constitution of crystalline and noncrystalline materials
        1.2.2   Stress and strain
        1.2.3   Elastic and plastic deformation; crack growth
    1.3   Sources of acoustic emission
        1.3.1   Burst emission, continuous emission
        1.3.2   Emission/signal levels, units of amplitude measurement
        1.3.3   Sources in crystalline materials
             1.3.3.1   Dislocations – plastic deformation
             1.3.3.2   Phase transformations
             1.3.3.3   Deformation twinning
             1.3.3.4   Nonmetallic inclusions
             1.3.3.5   Subcritical crack growth
                  1.3.3.5.1   Subcritical crack growth under increasing load
                  1.3.3.5.2   Ductile tearing under increasing load
                  1.3.3.5.3   Fatigue crack initiation and growth
                  1.3.3.5.4   Hydrogen embrittlement cracking
                  1.3.3.5.5   Stress corrosion cracking
        1.3.4   Sources in nonmetals
             1.3.4.1   Microcracking
             1.3.4.2   Gross cracking
             1.3.4.3   Crazing
             1.3.4.4   Other sources in nonmetals

Acoustic Emission Technique Course

4.2.5   Bucket trucks
4.2.6   Aircraft
4.2.7   Bridges
4.2.8   Mines
4.2.9   Dams, earthen slopes
4.2.10 Pumps, valves, etc.
4.2.11 Rotating plant
4.2.12 In-process weld monitoring
4.2.13 Leak detection and monitoring
4.2.14 Other structural applications

Acoustic Emission Testing Level III Topical Outline

1.0   Principles and Theory
    1.1   Characteristics of acoustic emission testing
        1.1.1   Concepts of source, propagation, loading, measurement, display, evaluation
        1.1.2   Proper selection of acoustic emission as technique of choice
            1.1.2.1   Differences between acoustic emission testing and other techniques
            1.1.2.2   Complementary roles of acoustic emission and other methods
            1.1.2.3   Potential or conflicting results between methods
            1.1.2.4   Factors that qualify/disqualify the use of acoustic emission testing
        1.1.3   Math review (exponents, logarithms, metric units and conversions)
    1.2   Materials and deformation
        1.2.1   Materials constitution
            1.2.1.1   Crystalline/noncrystalline
            1.2.1.2   Metals/composites/other
        1.2.2   Stress and strain (including triaxial, residual, thermal)
        1.2.3   Elastic and plastic deformation; crack growth
        1.2.4   Materials properties (strength, toughness, etc.)
    1.3   Sources of acoustic emission
        1.3.1   Broadband nature of source spectra
        1.3.2   Emission/signal levels, units of amplitude measurement
        1.3.3   Sources in crystalline materials
            1.3.3.1   Dislocations – plastic deformation
            1.3.3.2   Phase transformations
            1.3.3.3   Deformation twinning
            1.3.3.4   Nonmetallic inclusions
            1.3.3.5   Subcritical crack growth
                1.3.3.5.1   Subcritical crack growth under increasing load
                1.3.3.5.2   Ductile tearing under increasing load
                1.3.3.5.3   Fatigue crack initiation and growth
                1.3.3.5.4   Hydrogen embrittlement cracking
                1.3.3.5.5   Stress corrosion cracking
        1.3.4   Sources in nonmetals
            1.3.4.1   Microcracking
            1.3.4.2   Gross cracking
            1.3.4.3   Crazing
            1.3.4.4   Other sources in nonmetals
        1.3.5   Sources in composites
            1.3.5.1   Fiber breakage
            1.3.5.2   Matrix cracking
            1.3.5.3   Fiber-matrix debonding
            1.3.5.4   Delamination
            1.3.5.5   Fiber pull-out, relaxation
            1.3.5.6   Friction
        1.3.6   Other sources

Training References
Acoustic Emission Testing, Level I, II and III

Annual Book of ASTM Standards, Volume 03.03, *Nondestructive Testing*. Philadelphia, PA: American Society for Testing and Materials. Latest edition.*

Bingham, A.H., C.W. Ek and J.R. Tanner, eds. *Acoustic Emission Testing of Aerial Devices and Associated Equipment used in the Utility Industries* – STP 1139. Philadelphia, PA: American Society for Testing and Materials. 1992.

Boiler and Pressure Vessel Code, Section V, Articles 11 and 12. New York, NY: American Society of Mechanical Engineers. Latest edition.

Drouillard, T. *Acoustic Emission: A Bibliography with Abstracts*. New York: Plenum Press. 1979.

Journal of Acoustic Emission. Volume 8, Number 1-2. Los Angeles, CA: Acoustic Emission Group. 1989.

Matthews, J.R. *Acoustic Emission (Nondestructive Testing Monographs and Tracts)*. New York: Gordon and Breach, Science Publishers, Inc. 1983.

Monitoring Structural Integrity by Acoustic Emission B STP 571. Philadelphia, PA: American Society for Testing and Materials. 1975.

Nicoll, A.R. *Acoustic Emission*. Germany: DGM Metallurgy Informationsgesellschaft. 1980.

Nondestructive Evaluation and Quality Control: ASM Handbook, Volume 17. Metals Park, OH: ASM International. 1989.*

Sachse, W., K. Yamaguchi and J. Roget, eds. *Acoustic Emission; Current Practice and Future Directions*, STP 1077. Philadelphia, PA: American Society for Testing and Materials. 1991.*

Spanner, J.C. *Acoustic Emission: Techniques and Applications*. Evanston, IL: Intex Publishing Co. 1974.

Supplement to Recommended Practice No. SNT-TC-1A (Q&A Book): Acoustic Emission Testing, Columbus, OH: The American Society for Nondestructive Testing, Inc. Latest Edition.*

Tracy, N., tech. ed., P.O. Moore, ed. *Nondestructive Testing Handbook*, third edition: Volume 6, *Acoustic Emission Testing*. Columbus, OH: The American Society for Nondestructive Testing, Inc. 2005.*

* Available from The American Society for Nondestructive Testing, Inc., Columbus, OH.

Alternating Current Field Measurement Testing Level I Topical Outline

Theory Course

1.0 Introduction to Electromagnetic Testing
    1.1 Brief history of testing
    1.2 Basic principles of NDT testing

2.0 Electromagnetic Theory
    2.1 Eddy current theory
        2.1.1 Generation of eddy currents by means of an AC field
        2.1.2 Effects of fields created by eddy currents
        2.1.3 Properties of eddy currents
            2.1.3.1 Travel in circular direction
            2.1.3.2 Eddy current distribution
            2.1.3.3 Effects of lift off and geometry
            2.1.3.4 Relationship of magnetic field in relation to a current in a coil

Technique Course

      5.2.1   Depth and length sizing capabilities
      5.2.2   Probe resolution
      5.2.3   Coating thickness

6.0   Scanning for Detection
   6.1   Initial set up
   6.2   Setting position indicators
   6.3   Probe orientation
   6.4   Scanning speed
   6.5   Scanning pattern for tubulars and pipes
   6.6   Scanning pattern for linear sections
   6.7   Scanning for transverse cracks

7.0   Signal Interpretation
   7.1   Review of display format
   7.2   Detection and examination procedure
   7.3   Crack signals – linear cracks, angled cracks, line contacts and multiple cracks, transverse cracks
   7.4   Other signal sources – lift-off, geometry, materials, magnetism, edges and corners

Alternating Current Field Measurement Testing Level II Topical Outline

Principles Course

1.0   Review of Electromagnetic Theory
   1.1   Eddy current theory
   1.2   Alternating current field measurement theory
   1.3   Types of alternating current field measurement sensing probes

2.0   Factors that Affect Depth of Penetration
   2.1   Conductivity
   2.2   Permeability
   2.3   Frequency
   2.4   Coil size

3.0   Factors that Affect Alternating Current Field Measurement Testing
   3.1   Residual fields
   3.2   Defect geometry
   3.3   Defect location: scanning pattern for attachments, corners and ratholes
   3.4   Defect orientation
   3.5   Distance between adjacent defects

Techniques and Applications Course

1.0   Software Commands
   1.1   Probe file production
      1.1.1   Selection of gain and frequency settings for specific applications
      1.1.2   Selection of current for specific applications
      1.1.3   Selections of sensitivity settings and scalings for specific applications
   1.2   Standardization settings
      1.2.1   Alarm settings
      1.2.2   Butterfly plot scalings
   1.3   Adjustment of communication rates

2.0 User Standards and Operating Procedures
    2.1 Explanation of standards applicable to alternating current field measurement testing
    2.2 Explanation of operating procedures applicable to alternating current field measurement testing

Eddy Current Testing Level I Topical Outline

Theory Course

1.0 Introduction to Eddy Current Testing
    1.1 Historical and developmental process
        1.1.1 Founding fathers: Arago, Lenz, Faraday, Maxwell
        1.1.2 Advances in electronics
    1.2 Basic physics and controlling principles
        1.2.1 Varying magnetic fields
        1.2.2 Electromagnetic induction
        1.2.3 Primary and secondary force relationships

2.0 Electromagnetic Theory
    2.1 Eddy current theory
        2.1.1 Generation of eddy currents by means of an AC field
        2.1.2 Effect of fields created by eddy currents (impedance changes)
        2.1.3 Effect of change of impedance on instrumentation
        2.1.4 Properties of eddy current
            2.1.4.1 Travel in circular direction
            2.1.4.2 Strongest on surface of test material
            2.1.4.3 Zero value at center of solid conductor placed in an alternating magnetic field
            2.1.4.4 Strength, time relationship and orientation as functions of test-system parameters and test-part characteristics
            2.1.4.5 Small magnitude of current flow
            2.1.4.6 Relationships of frequency and phase
            2.1.4.7 Electrical effects, conductivity of materials
            2.1.4.8 Magnetic effects, permeability of materials
            2.1.4.9 Geometrical effects

3.0 Lab Demonstration
    3.1 Generation of Z-curves with conductivity samples
    3.2 Generation of lift-off curves

Basic Technique Course

1.0 Types of Eddy Current Sensing Elements
    1.1 Probes
        1.1.1 Types of arrangements
            1.1.1.1 Probe coils
            1.1.1.2 Encircling coils
            1.1.1.3 Inside coils
        1.1.2 Modes of operation
            1.1.2.1 Absolute
            1.1.2.2 Differential
            1.1.2.3 Hybrids
        1.1.3 Theory of operation
        1.1.4 Hall effect sensors
            1.1.4.1 Theory of operation
            1.1.4.2 Differences between coil and hall-element systems

      1.1.5   Applications
           1.1.5.1   Measurement of material properties
           1.1.5.2   Flaw detection
           1.1.5.3   Geometrical features
      1.1.6   Advantages
      1.1.7   Limitations
  1.2   Factors affecting choice of sensing elements
      1.2.1   Type of part to be inspected
      1.2.2   Type of discontinuity to be detected
      1.2.3   Speed of testing required
      1.2.4   Amount of testing (percentage) required
      1.2.5   Probable location of discontinuity

2.0   Selection of Inspection Parameters
  2.1   Frequency
  2.2   Coil drive: current/voltage
  2.3   Hall element drive: current/voltage
  2.4   Channel gain
  2.5   Display sensitivity selections
  2.6   Standardization
  2.7   Filtering
  2.8   Thresholds

3.0   Readout Mechanisms
  3.1   Calibrated or uncalibrated meters
  3.2   Impedance plane displays
      3.2.1   Analog
      3.2.2   Digital
  3.3   Data recording systems
  3.4   Alarms, lights, etc.
  3.5   Numerical readouts
  3.6   Marking systems
  3.7   Sorting gates and tables
  3.8   Cutoff saw or shears
  3.9   Automation and feedback

4.0   Lab Demonstration
  4.1   Demo filter effects on rotating reference standards
  4.2   Demo lift-off effects
  4.3   Demo frequency effects
  4.4   Demo rotational and forward speed effects
  4.5   Generate a Z-curve with conductivity standards

Eddy Current Testing Level II Topical Outline

Principles Course

1.0   Review of Electromagnetic Theory
  1.1   Eddy current theory
  1.2   Types of eddy current sensing probes

2.0   Factors That Affect Coil Impedance
  2.1   Test part
      2.1.1   Conductivity
      2.1.2   Permeability
      2.1.3   Mass
      2.1.4   Homogeneity

2.2 Test system
    2.2.1 Frequency
    2.2.2 Coupling
    2.2.3 Field strength
    2.2.4 Test coil and shape
    2.2.5 Hall elements

3.0 Signal-to-Noise Ratio
    3.1 Definition
    3.2 Relationship to eddy current testing
    3.3 Methods of improving signal-to-noise ratio

4.0 Selection of Test Frequency
    4.1 Relationship of frequency to type of test
    4.2 Considerations affecting choice of test
        4.2.1 Signal-to-noise ratio
        4.2.2 Causes of noise
        4.2.3 Methods to reduce noise
            4.2.3.1 DC saturation
            4.2.3.2 Shielding
            4.2.3.3 Grounding
        4.2.4 Phase discrimination
        4.2.5 Response speed
        4.2.6 Skin effect

5.0 Coupling
    5.1 Fill factor
    5.2 Lift-off

6.0 Field Strength and its Selection
    6.1 Permeability changes
    6.2 Saturation
    6.3 Effect of AC field strength on eddy current testing

7.0 Instrument Design Considerations
    7.1 Amplification
    7.2 Phase detection
    7.3 Differentiation of filtering

Techniques and Applications Course

1.0 User Standards and Operating Procedures
    1.1 Explanation of standards and specifications used in eddy current testing

2.0 Inspection System Output
    2.1 Accept/reject criteria
        2.1.1 Sorting, go/no-go
    2.2 Signal classification processes
        2.2.1 Discontinuity
        2.2.2 Flaw
    2.3 Detection of signals of interest
        2.3.1 Near surface
        2.3.2 Far surface
    2.4 Flaw sizing techniques
        2.4.1 Phase to depth
        2.4.2 Volts to depth
    2.5 Calculation of flaw frequency
    2.6 Sorting for properties related to conductivity

2.7 Thickness evaluation
2.8 Measurement of ferromagnetic properties
    2.8.1 Comparative circuits

Remote Field Testing Level I Topical Outline

Theory Course

1.0 Introduction to Remote Field Testing
    1.1 Historical and developmental process
        1.1.1 Founding fathers: McLean, Schmidt, Atherton and Lord
        1.1.2 The computer age and its effect on the advancement of remote field testing (RFT)
    1.2 Basic physics and controlling principles
        1.2.1 Varying magnetic fields
        1.2.2 Electromagnetic induction
        1.2.3 Primary and secondary field relationships

2.0 Electromagnetic Theory
    2.1 Generation of eddy currents in conductors
    2.2 Eddy current propagation and decay, standard depth of penetration
    2.3 Near field, transition and remote field zones
    2.4 Properties of remote field eddy currents
        2.4.1 Through-transmission nature
        2.4.2 Magnetic flux is predominant energy
        2.4.3 The ferrous tube as a wave guide
        2.4.4 Strength of field in three zones
        2.4.5 External field is source of energy in remote field
        2.4.6 Factors affecting phase lag and amplitude
        2.4.7 Geometric factors: fill factor, external support plates, tube sheets
        2.4.8 Speed of test, relationship to thickness, frequency, conductivity and permeability
        2.4.9 Effect of deposits, magnetite, copper, calcium
        2.4.10 Remote field testing (RFT) in nonferrous tubes

Basic Technique Course

1.0 Types of Remote Field Sensing Elements
    1.1 Probes
        1.1.1 Types of arrangements
            1.1.1.1 Absolute bobbin coils
            1.1.1.2 Differential bobbin coils
            1.1.1.3 Arrays
        1.1.2 Modes of operation
            1.1.2.1 RFT voltage plane and reference curve
            1.1.2.2 X-Y voltage plane
            1.1.2.3 Chart recordings
        1.1.3 Theory of operation
        1.1.4 Applications
            1.1.4.1 Heat exchanger and boiler tubes
            1.1.4.2 Pipes and pipelines
            1.1.4.3 External and through-transmission probes
        1.1.5 Advantages
            1.1.5.1 Equal sensitivity to internal and external flaws
            1.1.5.2 Easy to understand: increasing depth of flaw signals rotate CCW
        1.1.6 Limitations

                1.1.6.1   Speed
                1.1.6.2   Difficult to differentiate internal versus external flaws
                1.1.6.3   Small signals from small volume flaws
                1.1.6.4   Finned tubes
    1.2   Factors affecting choice of probe type
        1.2.1   Differential for small volume flaws (e.g. pits)
        1.2.2   Absolute for large area defects (e.g. steam erosion, fretting)
        1.2.3   Test (probe travel) speed
        1.2.4   Single versus dual exciters and areas of reduced sensitivity
        1.2.5   Bobbin coils and solid state sensors
        1.2.6   Finned tubes

2.0   Selection of Inspection Parameters
    2.1   Frequency
    2.2   Coil drive: current/voltage
    2.3   Pre-amp gain
    2.4   Display gain
    2.5   Standardization

3.0   Readout Mechanisms
    3.1   Display types:
        3.1.1   RFT voltage plane displays
        3.1.2   Voltage vector displays
    3.2   RFT reference curve
    3.3   Chart recordings
    3.4   Odometers
    3.5   Storing and recalling data on computers

Principles Course

1.0   Review of Electromagnetic Theory
    1.1   RFT theory
    1.2   Types of RFT sensing probes

2.0   Factors That Affect Coil Impedance
    2.1   Test part
        2.1.1   Conductivity
        2.1.2   Permeability
        2.1.3   Mass
        2.1.4   Homogeneity
    2.2   Test system
        2.2.1   Frequency
        2.2.2   Coupling (fill factor)
        2.2.3   Field strength (drive volts, frequency)
        2.2.4   Coil shapes

3.0   Signal-to-Noise Ratio
    3.1   Definition
    3.2   Relationship to RFT testing
    3.3   Methods of improving signal-to-noise ratio:
        3.3.1   Speed
        3.3.2   Fill factor
        3.3.3   Frequency
        3.3.4   Filters
        3.3.5   Drive
        3.3.6   Shielding
        3.3.7   Grounding [(6) and (7) also apply to other methods]

4.0 Selection of Test Frequency
    4.1   Relationship of frequency to depth of penetration
    4.2   Relationship of frequency to resolution
    4.3   Dual frequency operation
    4.4   Beat frequencies
    4.5   Optimum frequency

5.0 Coupling
    5.1   Fill factor
    5.2   Importance of centralizing the probe

6.0 Field Strength
    6.1   Probe drive and penetration
    6.2   Effect of increasing thickness, conductivity or permeability
    6.3   Position of receive coils versus field strength

7.0 Instrument Design Considerations
    7.1   Amplification
    7.2   Phase and amplitude detection (lock-in amplifier)
    7.3   Differentiation and filtering

Remote Field Testing Level II Topical Outline

Techniques and Applications Course

1.0 Equipment
    1.1   Probes
        1.1.1   Absolute bobbin coils
        1.1.2   Differential bobbin coils
        1.1.3   Arrays
        1.1.4   Dual exciter or dual detector probes
        1.1.5   Solid state sensors
        1.1.6   External probes
        1.1.7   Effect of fill factor
        1.1.8   Centralizing the probe
        1.1.9   Quality of the "ride"
        1.1.10 Cable length considerations
        1.1.11 Pre-amps internal and external
    1.2   Instruments
        1.2.1   Measuring phase and amplitude
        1.2.2   Displays: remote field testing (RFT), voltage plane, impedance plane differences
        1.2.3   Chart recordings
        1.2.4   Storing, retrieving, archiving data
        1.2.5   Standardization frequency
    1.3   Reference standards
        1.3.1   Material
        1.3.2   Thickness
        1.3.3   Size
        1.3.4   Heat treatment
        1.3.5   Simulated defects
        1.3.6   ASTM E 2096
        1.3.7   How often to standardize

2.0 Techniques
    2.1   Factors affecting signals
        2.1.1   Probe speed/smoothness of travel
        2.1.2   Depth, width and length of flaw versus probe footprint

Electromagnetic Testing Level III Topical Outline

Eddy Current Testing

1.0 Principles/Theory
    1.1   Eddy current theory
        1.1.1   Generation of eddy currents
        1.1.2   Effect of fields created by eddy currents (impedance changes)
        1.1.3   Properties of eddy currents
            1.1.3.1   Travel mode
            1.1.3.2   Depth of penetration
            1.1.3.3   Effects of test part characteristics – conductivity and permeability
            1.1.3.4   Current flow
            1.1.3.5   Frequency and phase
            1.1.3.6   Effects of permeability variations – noise
            1.1.3.7   Effects of discontinuity orientation

2.0 Equipment/Materials
    2.1   Probes – general
        2.1.1   Advantages/limitations
    2.2   Through, encircling or annular coils and hall elements
        2.2.1   Advantages/limitations/differences
    2.3   Factors affecting choice of sensing elements
        2.3.1   Type of part to be inspected
        2.3.2   Type of discontinuity to be detected
        2.3.3   Speed of testing required
        2.3.4   Amount of testing required
        2.3.5   Probable location of discontinuity
        2.3.6   Applications other than discontinuity detection
    2.4   Read out selection
        2.4.1   Meter
        2.4.2   Oscilloscope, X-Y and other displays
        2.4.3   Alarm, lights, etc.
        2.4.4   Strip chart recorder
    2.5   Instrument design considerations
        2.5.1   Amplification
        2.5.2   Phase detection
        2.5.3   Differentiation or filtering
        2.5.4   Thresholds, box gates, etc.

3.0 Techniques/Calibrations
    3.1   Factors which affect coil impedance
        3.1.1   Test part
        3.1.2   Test system
    3.2   Selection of test frequency
        3.2.1   Relation of frequency to type of test
        3.2.2   Consideration affecting choice of test
            3.2.2.1   Signal/noise ratio
            3.2.2.2   Phase discrimination
            3.2.2.3   Response speed
            3.2.2.4   Skin effect
    3.3   Coupling
        3.3.1   Fill factor
        3.3.2   Lift-off
    3.4   Field strength
        3.4.1   Permeability changes
        3.4.2   Saturation
        3.4.3   Effect of AC field strength on eddy current testing

Remote Field Testing

Alternating Current Field Measurement Testing

1.0 Principles and Theory
    1.1 Generation of eddy currents
    1.2 Effect of fields created by eddy currents
    1.3 Properties of eddy currents
        1.3.1 Depth of penetration
        1.3.2 Effects of test part characteristics
        1.3.3 Current flow
        1.3.4 Frequency
        1.3.5 Effects of permeability variations
        1.3.6 Effects of discontinuity orientation

2.0 Equipment and Materials
    2.1 Alternating current measurement probes general
        2.1.1 Advantages and limitations
    2.2 Factors affecting choice of probes
        2.2.1 Type of part to be inspected
        2.2.2 Type of discontinuity to be inspected
        2.2.3 Speed of testing required
        2.2.4 Amount of testing required
        2.2.5 Probable location of discontinuity
        2.2.6 Applications other that discontinuity detection
    2.3 Techniques/equipment sensitivity
        2.3.1 Selection of test frequency
        2.3.2 Selection of correct probe scalings in relation to the test
        2.3.3 Selection of correct communication rates

3.0 Interpretation and Evaluation of Signals
    3.1 Flaw detection

4.0 Procedures

Training References
Electromagnetic Testing Method, Level I, II and III

Annual Book of ASTM Standards, Volume 03.03 *Nondestructive Testing.* Philadelphia, PA: American Society for Testing and Materials. Latest edition.*

ASNT Level III Study Guide: Electromagnetic Testing. Columbus, OH: The American Society for Nondestructive Testing, Inc. Latest edition.*

ASTM E690 - 10 Standard Practice for In Situ Electromagnetic (Eddy-Current) Examination of Nonmagnetic Heat Exchanger Tubes. West Conshohocken, PA: ASTM International. 2010.**

Beissner, R.E., G.A. Matzkanin, C.M. Teller. NTIAC-80-1, *NDE Applications of Magnetic Leakage Field Methods,* January 1980.

Bray, D.E. and D. McBride. *Nondestructive Testing Techniques.* New York, NY: John Wiley & Sons. 1992.

Cecco, V.S., G. Van Drunen and F.L. Sharp. *Eddy Current Testing,* US Edition, Columbia, MD: Nichols Publishing, Inc. 1987 (AECL-7523).*

Kilgore, R.J. and S. Ramchandran. "Remote Field Eddy Current Testing of Small-Diameter Carbon Steel Tubes," *Materials Evaluation.* Vol. 47, No.1. 1989. pp 32-36.*

Libby, H.L. *Introduction to Electromagnetic Nondestructive Test Methods.* Huntington, NY: Robert E. Krieger Publishing Co. 1979.

Mackintosh, D.D., D.L. Atherton and P.A. Puhach. "Through-Transmission Equations for Remote-Field Eddy Current Inspection of Small Bore Ferromagnetic Tubes," *Materials Evaluation*. Vol. 51, No. 6. 1993. pp 744-748.*

Mackintosh, D.D., D.L. Atherton, T.R. Schmidt and D.E. Russell. "Back to Basics: Remote Field Eddy Current for Examination of Ferromagnetic Tubes," *Materials Evaluation*. Vol. 54, No. 6. 1996. pp 652-657.*

Materials and Processes for NDT Technology. Columbus, OH: The American Society for Nondestructive Testing, Inc. 1981.*

Mordfin, L. *Handbook of Reference Data for Nondestructive Testing*. second edition, West Conshohocken, PA: ASTM International. 2002.**

Sadek, H. *Electromagnetic Testing Classroom Training Book* (PTP Series). Columbus, OH: The American Society for Nondestructive Testing, Inc. 2006.*

Schmidt, T.R. "History of The Remote Field Eddy Current Inspection Technique," *Materials Evaluation*. Vol. 42, No. 1. 1984. pp 14-22.*

Schmidt, T.R. "The Remote Field Eddy Current Technique," *Materials Evaluation*. Vol. 42, No. 2. 1984. pp 223-230.*

Schmidt, T.R., D.L. Atherton, and S. Sullivan. "Back to Basics: The Remote-Field Transition Zone," *Materials Evaluation*. Vol. 47, No. 9. 1989. pp 969-100.*

Smith, H. and D.D. Mackintosh. *Remote Field Eddy Current Examination of Boiler Tubes*. Proceedings of EPRI Topical Workshop on Electromagnetic NDE Applications in the Electric Power Industry, Charlotte, NC, August 21-23, 1995. pp 1-17.

Sollish, D.B. *Field Experience in Boiler Examinations Using Remote Field Eddy Current*. Corrosion 91: NACE Annual Conference and Corrosion Show, Cincinnati, OH, March 11-15, 1991. pp 224/1 to 224/8.

Sullivan, S. and D.L. Atherton. "Analysis of the Remote Field Eddy Current Effect in Nonmagnetic Tubes," *Materials Evaluation*. Vol. 47, No. 1. 1989. pp 80-86.*

Supplement to Recommended Practice No. SNT-TC-1A (Q&A Book): Electromagnetic Testing Method. Columbus, OH: The American Society for Nondestructive Testing, Inc. Latest edition.*

Taylor, J.L., ed. *Basic Metallurgy for Non-Destructive Testing*, revised edition. Essex, England: W.H. Houldershaw, Ltd. (British Institute of Nondestructive Testing) 1988.*

Udpa, S., tech. ed., P.O. Moore, ed. *Nondestructive Testing Handbook,* third edition: Volume 5, *Electromagnetic Testing*. Columbus, OH: American Society for Nondestructive Testing, Inc., 2004.*

The following selected papers are available from PCN Certification Services, British Institute of NDT, 1 Spencer Parade, Northampton NN1 5AA. The list of available papers may be extended by the addition of later publications. This document will not be revised to show the extended list in every case.

Raine, A. and C. Laenen. "Additional Applications with the Alternating Current Field Measurement (ACFM) Technique," Proceedings of the ASNT Spring Conference and 7th Annual Research Symposium, March 1998.

Topp, D. "The Alternating Current Field Measurement Technique and its Application to the Inspection of Oil and Gas Installations," 32nd Annual British Institute of NDT Conference (*Insight*. Vol. 36, No.6. June 1994).

Raine, A. "An Alternative Method for Offshore Inspection," CSNDT Annual Conference. 1995. (*Insight*. Vol. 36, No. 9. September 1994).

B53683 Part 5: Terms Used in Eddy Current.

Lugg, M. *An Introduction to Alternating Current Field Measurement*.

Topp, D. and B. Jones. *Operational Experience with the ACFM Inspection Technique for Subsea Weld Inspection*. British Gas Environmental Engineering, March 1994.

PCN Classroom Training Handbook – Product Technology (PCN Certification Services, British Institute of NDT).

Collins, R. and M.C. Lugg. "Use of AC Field Measurements for Non-Destructive Testing," *Fatigue Crack Measurement: Techniques and Applications*. Engineering Materials Advisory Services, Ltd. 1991.

Topp, O. *The Use of Manual and Automated Alternating Current Field Measurement Techniques for Subsea and Topside Crack Detection and Sizing*. Offshore S E Asia, December 1994, OSEA 94.137.

*   Available from The American Society for Nondestructive Testing, Inc., Columbus OH.

**   Available from The American Society for Testing of Materials.

Ground Penetrating Radar Level I Topical Outline

Theory Course

1.0   Introduction to Ground Penetrating Radar (GPR)
      1.1   Radar
           1.1.1   Reflection
           1.1.2   Radar equation
           1.1.3   Polarization
           1.1.4   Interference
      1.2   The history of GPR

2.0   Electromagnetic Theory
      2.1   Electromagnetic wave propagation
      2.2   Velocity
      2.3   Wavelength
      2.4   Interference
           2.4.1   Attenuation
           2.4.2   Dispersion
           2.4.3   Noise
           2.4.4   Clutter
      2.5   Electrical properties
           2.5.1   Relative dielectric permittivity
           2.5.2   Electrical conductivity
           2.5.3   Dielectric materials
                 2.5.3.1   Conductors
                 2.5.3.2   Insulators
                 2.5.3.3   Semiconductors
           2.5.4   Types of materials
                 2.5.4.1   Soil
                 2.5.4.2   Concrete
                 2.5.4.3   Rocks
                 2.5.4.4   Water – salt/fresh
                 2.5.4.5   Ice
                 2.5.4.6   Others
      2.6   Magnetic properties in materials
           2.6.1   Ferromagnetic
           2.6.2   Ferrimagnetic
           2.6.3   Super paramagnetic

3.0   GPR Equipment
      3.1   Antennas
           3.1.1   Polarization
           3.1.2   Fresnel reflection
           3.1.3   Snell angle
           3.1.4   Near field/far field
           3.1.5   Frequencies

3.2 Coupling
    3.2.1 Impedance matching
    3.2.2 Unloading
    3.2.3 Ringing
3.3 Waveguides

Basic Techniques Course

1.0 Surveys
  1.1 Defining the objectives
  1.2 Antenna selection and orientation
    1.2.1 Speed
    1.2.2 Frequency
    1.2.3 Application
    1.2.4 Materials
    1.2.5 Targets
  1.3 Depth of penetration
    1.3.1 Gain controls
    1.3.2 Sensitivity controls
    1.3.3 Calibration
  1.4 Range settings
  1.5 Filter settings
  1.6 Scanning parameters
    1.6.1 Mapping
    1.6.2 Grid layout
    1.6.3 Spacing

2.0 Applications
  2.1 Test methods
  2.2 Advantages
  2.3 Limitations

3.0 Data Display and Interpretation
  3.1 Material properties
  3.2 Layer reflection
    3.2.1 Trench effect
  3.3 Target reflection
    3.3.1 Point targets
  3.4 Detection accuracy
  3.5 Horizontal accuracy and resolution
  3.6 Depth accuracy and resolution
  3.7 Measurement techniques

Ground Penetrating Radar Level II Topical Outline

Principles and Applications Course

1.0 Review of Electromagnetic Theory
  1.1 Radar equation
  1.2 Stokes vector
  1.3 Mueller matrix
  1.4 Poincaré sphere

2.0 Types of Tests

3.0 Factors Affecting Tests
    3.1   Depth of investigation
    3.2   Orientation
    3.3   Noise
        3.3.1   Signal-to-noise ratios
        3.3.2   Causes
        3.3.3   Filters
    3.4   Interferences
    3.5   Noninvasive surfaces

4.0 Field Strength
    4.1   Antenna drive
    4.2   Effects of conductivity
    4.3   Permeability effects
    4.4   Ground truth
    4.5   Hyperbolic shape analysis

5.0 Instrument Design Considerations
    5.1   Waveguides
    5.2   Multipathing
    5.3   Near field and far field factors
    5.4   Resonance
    5.5   Resolution

6.0 Data
    6.1   Data acquisition
    6.2   Data processing
        6.2.1   Displays
    6.3   Modeling
    6.4   Interpretation
        6.4.1   Uncertainty

Ground Penetrating Radar Level III Topical Outline

Theory Course

1.0 Introduction
    1.1   History
    1.2   Applications

2.0 Systems Design
    2.1   Range
        2.1.1   Antenna loss
        2.1.2   Transmission loss
        2.1.3   Coupling loss
        2.1.4   Mismatch
        2.1.5   Target scatter
        2.1.6   Material attenuation
    2.2   Velocity propagation
    2.3   Clutter
    2.4   Resolution
        2.4.1   Depth
        2.4.2   Plan

3.0 Modeling
    3.1   Time domain models
    3.2   Antenna radiation

Applications Course

Training References
Ground Penetrating Radar Method, Level I, II and III

Daniels, D., ed., *Ground Penetrating Radar*, second edition. London, UK: The Institution of Engineering and Technology. 2004.

Jol, H.M. ed. *Ground Penetrating Radar Theory and Applications*. Oxford, UK: Elsevier Science. 2009.

Laser Testing Methods – Holography/Shearography Testing Level I Topical Outline

Basic Holography/Shearography Physics Course

Note: It is recommended that the trainee receive instruction in this course, which focuses on laser safety, prior to performing work in holography and shearography.

1.0 Introduction
    1.1   Definition of speckle interferometry
    1.2   History of holography and shearography testing
    1.3   Applications of shearography NDT (SNDT)
    1.4   Nondestructive testing
    1.5   Responsibilities of levels of certificatio
    1.6   Overview of shearography NDT

2.0 Basic Principles of Light and SNDT
    2.1   Nature of light
    2.2   Light as a wave
    2.3   Definition of coherence
    2.4   Speckle
    2.5   Interference
    2.6   Interferometry
    2.7   Stress, the application of force
    2.8   Strain, the resultant deformation
    2.9   The double lobed fringe pattern

3.0 Lasers
    3.1   Introduction to lasers
    3.2   Laser light
    3.3   Expanded coherent light as a measuring stick
    3.4   Types of lasers
    3.5   Ion lasers
    3.6   Diode lasers

4.0 Laser Safety
    4.1   Introduction
    4.2   Dangers of intra-beam viewing
    4.3   Classifications of laser systems
    4.4   Nature of laser light
    4.5   The expanded beam
    4.6   Laser measurements for safety
    4.7   Safe use of lasers
    4.8   Laser safety officer
    4.9   Safety requirements for the laboratory
    4.10   Safety requirements for production
    4.11   Safety requirements for the shop or field
    4.12   Safe system design
    4.13   Enclosures
    4.14   Interlocks
    4.15   Safety during maintenance
    4.16   Keeping laser systems safe

5.0 Basic Holography/Shearography System
    5.1   Laser illumination
    5.2   Shearography camera

Basic Operating Course

Basic Application Course

8.0 Vibration Excitation, Acoustic
    8.1 Types of excitation
        8.1.1 Frequency versus material
        8.1.2 Frequency versus defect size
        8.1.3 Amplitude
        8.1.4 White noise
    8.2 Phase reversing
    8.3 Applications
    8.4 Interpretation of results
    8.5 Safe use of acoustic exciters

9.0 Complex Structures
    9.1 Types of constructions
    9.2 Interpretation of results

Holography/Shearography Testing Level II Topical Outline

Intermediate Physics Course

1.0 Physics of Light
    1.1 Basic wave theory
    1.2 Coherence and interference
    1.3 Specular versus diffuse light
    1.4 Holography optics (in-plane and out-of-plane)
    1.5 Shearography optics

2.0 Physics of Lasers
    2.1 Construction of ion lasers
    2.2 Maintenance of ion lasers
    2.3 Fiber optic beam delivery systems
    2.4 Construction of DPY lasers
    2.5 Logistics and choice of lasers

3.0 Laser Safety Officer
    3.1 The guide to the safe use of lasers
    3.2 Developing procedures

4.0 Physics of Materials
    4.1 Stress/strain, the modulus of elasticity
    4.2 Plate deformation equation
    4.3 Deformation versus strain
    4.4 Specular versus diffuse materials
    4.5 Transparent and translucent materials
    4.6 Mechanical stress/strain
    4.7 Thermal expansion of materials
    4.8 Vacuum stress and out-of-plane strain
    4.9 Pressure, axial and hoop strain
    4.10 Vibration and resonance
    4.11 Stress relaxation

Intermediate Operating Course

1.0 Holography and Shearography Systems
    1.1 Automated inspection stations
    1.2 Tripod-based inspections
    1.3 On vehicle inspections

2.0 Sources of Noise and Solutions
    2.1 Stability
    2.2 Vibration
    2.3 Thermal gradients
    2.4 Air currents

3.0 Fixturing
    3.1 Simple forms
    3.2 Automated system requirements

4.0 Speckle Interferometry Camera
    4.1 Field of view (FOV)
    4.2 Resolution versus FOV
    4.3 Focus and iris settings
    4.4 Sensitivity versus shear angle
    4.5 In-plane, out-of-plane considerations
    4.6 Effects of shear orientation
    4.7 Specular reflections

5.0 Speckle Interferometry – Image Processor
    5.1 Advanced processor adjustment
    5.2 Advanced post-processing techniques
    5.3 Interface options
    5.4 Documentation options

6.0 Stressing Systems, Setup and Operation
    6.1 Thermal stressing system
    6.2 Vacuum inspection station
    6.3 Pressurization stressing
    6.4 Vibration excitation

7.0 Method Development
    7.1 Test standards
    7.2 Method format

8.0 Documentation
    8.1 Digital image file management
    8.2 Reporting
    8.3 Video prints
    8.4 Videotapes
    8.5 Archiving data

Intermediate Applications Course

1.0 Materials and Applications
    1.1 Laminates
    1.2 Honeycombs
    1.3 Foam core materials
    1.4 Advanced materials
    1.5 Pressure vessel, piping and tubing
    1.6 Plasma spray and ceramics
    1.7 Bonded metal

2.0 Fringe Interpretation
    2.1 Quantitative fringe measurement
    2.2 Defect measurement and characterization
    2.3 Strain measurement

3.0　Mechanical Loading
    3.1　Review of mechanical loading methods
    3.2　Applications
        3.2.1　Cracks
        3.2.2　Material weaknesses
        3.2.3　Interpretation of results

4.0　Thermal Stress
    4.1　Review of thermal stressing methods
        4.1.1　Time versus temperature
        4.1.2　Time versus depth
    4.2　Applications
        4.2.1　Delamination
        4.2.2　Impact damage
        4.2.3　Composite repair evaluation
        4.2.4　Foreign material
    4.3　Interpretation of results

5.0　Vacuum Stress
    5.1　Review of vacuum stressing methods
        5.1.1　The general purpose method
        5.1.2　Depth versus fringes
    5.2　Applications
        5.2.1　Near side disbonds
        5.2.2　Far side disbonds
        5.2.3　Composite repair evaluation
        5.2.4　Delaminations
    5.3　Interpretation of results
        5.3.1　Effects of windows

6.0　Pressurization Stress
    6.1　Review of pressure stressing methods
    6.2　Applications
        6.2.1　Piping and tubing
        6.2.2　Pressure vessels
        6.2.3　Aircraft fuselage
    6.3　Interpretation of results

7.0　Vibration Excitation, Mechanical
    7.1　Review of mechanical vibration excitation methods
        7.1.1　Frequency versus material
        7.1.2　Frequency versus defect size
        7.1.3　Amplitude
        7.1.4　Sweep rate
        7.1.5　White noise
    7.2　Applications
    7.3　Interpretation of results

8.0　Vibration Excitation, Acoustic
    8.1　Review of acoustic vibration excitation methods
        8.1.1　Frequency versus material
        8.1.2　Frequency versus defect size
        8.1.3　Amplitude
        8.1.4　Sweep rate
        8.1.5　White noise
    8.2　Applications
    8.3　Interpretation of results
    8.4　Safe use of acoustic exciters

9.0 Other Stressing Methods
    9.1   Review of stress relaxation methods
    9.2   Applications
    9.3   Interpretation

Laser Methods Holography/Shearography Testing Level III Topical Outline

1.0   Principles/Theory
    1.1   Light
        1.1.1   Light and basic wave theory
        1.1.2   Coherence and interference
        1.1.3   Electronic speckle
        1.1.4   Speckle interferometry
    1.2   Lasers
        1.2.1   Laser principles
        1.2.2   Properties of laser light
        1.2.3   Laser light as a measurement tool
        1.2.4   Ion lasers
        1.2.5   Diode lasers
    1.3   Optics
        1.3.1   Holographic optics
        1.3.2   Shearography optics
        1.3.3   Polarization
        1.3.4   Filters
    1.4   Material properties
        1.4.1   Stress/strain, the modulus of elasticity
        1.4.2   Plate deformation equation
        1.4.3   Deformation versus strain
        1.4.4   Specular versus diffuse reflections
        1.4.5   Transparent and translucent materials
        1.4.6   Thermal expansion of materials
        1.4.7   Vacuum stress and out-of-plane strain
        1.4.8   Pressure, axial and hoop strain
        1.4.9   Vibration and resonance
        1.4.10 Stress relaxation

2.0   Equipment/Materials
    2.1   Holographic systems
        2.1.1   Fundamentals of holography
        2.1.2   Holographic instruments
        2.1.3   Interpreting results
    2.2   Shearographic systems
        2.2.1   Image subtraction correlation systems
        2.2.2   Phase stepping systems
        2.2.3   Production systems
        2.2.4   Automated systems
        2.2.5   Field inspection systems
    2.3   Basic setup
        2.3.1   Illumination
             2.3.1.1   Illumination versus field of view
             2.3.1.2   Laser speckle considerations
             2.3.1.3   In-plane, out-of-plane considerations
        2.3.2   Fixturing
             2.3.2.1   Simple forms
             2.3.2.2   Automated system requirements

Training References
Holography/Shearography Testing, Level I, II and III

Spicer, J.W.M., J.L. Champion, R. Osiander and J. Spicer. *Thermal Stressing Techniques for Flaw Characterization with Shearography*, SPIE Vol. 2455. 1995. pp. 250-259.

Stanley, R.K., tech. ed., P. McIntire and P.O. Moore, eds. *Nondestructive Testing Handbook*, second edition, Volume 9, *Special Nondestructive Testing Method*s. Columbus, OH: The American Society for Nondestructive Testing, Inc. 1995.*

Tyson, J. *Advances in Evaluation of Composites and Composite Repairs*. Proc. SAMPE. 1995. pp. 71-78.

Tyson, J. "Full-field Vibration and Strain Measurement," *Sensors, The Journal of Applied Sensing Technology*. Vol. 16, No. 6, June 1999. pp. 16-22.

Tyson, J., R. Wegner and A. Ettemeyer. "Non-contact Total Strain Measurement for Failure Prediction," *Materials Evaluation*. Vol. 57, No. 6. 1999. pp. 576-580.*

*   Available from The American Society for Nondestructive Testing, Inc., Columbus OH.

Laser Testing – Profilometry
Level I Topical Outline

1.0 Introduction
    1.1 Brief history of NDT and laser methods testing
    1.2 Purpose for laser profilometry testing
    1.3 Benefits and limitations of laser profilometry testing

2.0 Lasers and Laser Safety
    2.1 Introduction to lasers
    2.2 Laser classifications
    2.3 Basic laser safety
    2.4 Precautions for safe laser operation
    2.5 Definitions

3.0 Theory of Laser Profilometry Testing
    3.1 Introduction to basic optical triangulation
    3.2 Photodetectors
    3.3 Calibration

4.0 Laser Profilometry Testing
    4.1 Preparation of test parts
    4.2 Environmental considerations and limitations
    4.3 System setup
    4.4 Instrument calibration
    4.5 Data acquisition
    4.6 Data storage

5.0 Introduction to Data Processing and Analysis
    5.1 Confirming quality of inspection results
    5.2 Basic interpretation of test results
    5.3 Data storage and archival

Laser Testing – Profilometry
Level II Topical Outline

1.0 Introduction
    1.1 Purpose for laser methods and laser profilometry testing
    1.2 Review of basic principles of laser profilometry testing
    1.3 Benefits and limitations of laser profilometry testing
    1.4 Responsibilities of Level II laser profilometry examiner
    1.5 Limitations of Level II laser profilometry examiner

2.0 Laser Safety
    2.1 Types laser types
    2.2 Laser classifications
    2.3 Laser safety equipment
    2.4 Precautions for safe laser operation
    2.5 Regulations and governing organizations

3.0 Intermediate Theory of Profilometry Testing
    3.1 Optical triangulation
    3.2 Lasers
        3.2.1 Gas lasers
        3.2.2 Diode lasers
    3.3 Lenses and optical filters

3.4 Photodetectors
    3.4.1 Charge couple devices
    3.4.2 Lateral effect photodetectors
3.5 Basic signal processing
3.6 Calibration

4.0 Conducting Laser Profilometry Inspection
    4.1 Equipment selection and setup
    4.2 Environmental considerations
        4.2.1 Test material
        4.2.2 Dust and other contamination
        4.2.3 Humidity and moisture
        4.2.4 Power considerations
    4.3 Calibration
        4.3.1 When to calibrate
        4.3.2 Factors that affect calibration
    4.4 Acquiring and saving inspection results

5.0 Evaluation of Indications
    5.1 General
        5.1.1 Flaws in various materials
        5.1.2 Overview of typical causes of flaws in materials
        5.1.3 Appearance of flaws
        5.1.4 Non-flaw-related indication
    5.2 Factors affecting quality of inspection results
        5.2.1 Condition/cleanliness of test component surface
        5.2.2 Reflectivity of test component surface
        5.2.3 Sharp corners/glints
        5.2.4 Signal too high/too low

6.0 Inspection Procedures and Standards
    6.1 Inspection procedures and specifications
    6.2 Standards
    6.3 Codes

Laser Testing – Profilometry
Level III Topical Outline

1.0 Introduction
    1.1 Purpose for laser methods and laser profilometry testing
    1.2 Responsibilities of Level III laser profilometry examiner
    1.3 Limitations of Level III laser profilometry examiner

2.0 Knowledge of Other Basic NDT methods
    2.1 Advantages and limitations of each method
    2.2 Applications well suited to laser profilometry testing
    2.3 Test methods that complement laser profilometry testing

3.0 Laser Safety
    3.1 Laser classifications
        3.1.1 Laser power calculation
        3.1.2 Calculating laser classification
    3.2 Precautions and equipment for safe laser operation
    3.3 Regulations and governing organizations
        3.3.1 Laser product user
        3.3.2 Laser product manufacturer

Training References
Laser-based Profilometry Testing, Level I, II and III

American National Standards Institute, *American National Standard for the Safe Use of Lasers: ANSI Z-136.1*, Orlando, FL: Laser Institute of America. Latest edition.

Bickel, G., G. Hausler and M. Maul. "Triangulation with Expanded Range of Depth," *Optical Engineering*. Vol. 24, No. 6. Bellingham, WA: International Society for Optical Engineering (Society of Photo-Optical Engineers). 1985. pp. 975-977.

Owen, R.B. and M.L. Awscock. "One and Two Dimensional Position Sensitive Photodetectors," *IEEE Transactions on Electron Devices*. Vol. ED-21, No. 3. New York, NY: Institute of Electrical and Electronic Engineers. 1968. pp. 290-297.

Stanley, R.K., tech. ed., P. McIntire and P.O. Moore, eds. *Nondestructive Testing Handbook*, second edition: Volume 9, *Special Nondestructive Testing Methods*. Section 3, Part 4, "Laser-based Profilometry Using Point Triangulation." Columbus, OH: American Society for Nondestructive Testing, Inc. 1995. pp 141-157.*

*   Available from The American Society for Nondestructive Testing, Inc., Columbus OH.

Leak Testing Level I Topical Outline

Fundamentals in Leak Testing Course

1.0   Introduction
    1.1   History of leak testing
    1.2   Reasons for leak testing
        1.2.1   Material loss prevention
        1.2.2   Contamination
        1.2.3   Component/system reliability
        1.2.4   Pressure-differential maintenance
        1.2.5   Personnel/public safety
    1.3   Functions of leak testing
        1.3.1   Categories
        1.3.2   Applications
    1.4   Training and certification

2.0   Leak Testing Fundamentals
    2.1   Terminology
        2.1.1   Leakage terms
        2.1.2   Leakage tightness
        2.1.3   Quantitative/semi-quantitative
        2.1.4   Sensitivity/calibration terms
    2.2   Leak testing units
        2.2.1   Mathematics in leak testing
        2.2.2   Exponential notation
        2.2.3   Basic and fundamental units
        2.2.4   The International System of Units (SI)
    2.3   Physical units in leak testing
        2.3.1   Volume and pressure
        2.3.2   Time and temperature
        2.3.3   Absolute values
        2.3.4   Standard or atmospheric conditions
        2.3.5   Leakage measurement
    2.4   Leak testing standards
        2.4.1   Capillary or permeation
        2.4.2   National Institute of Standards and Technology (NIST) standards
        2.4.3   System versus instrument calibration
        2.4.4   Inaccuracy of calibration
    2.5   Flow characteristics
        2.5.1   Gas flow
        2.5.2   Liquid flow
        2.5.3   Correlation of leakage rates
        2.5.4   Anomalous leaks
        2.5.5   Leak clogging
    2.6   Vacuum fundamentals
        2.6.1   Introduction to vacuum
            2.6.1.1   Terminology
            2.6.1.2   Principles
            2.6.1.3   Units of pressure

Safety in Leak Testing Course

Note: It is recommended that the trainee, as well as all other leak testing personnel, receive instruction in this course prior to performing work in leak testing.

3.0 Pressure Precautions
    3.1 Pressure test versus proof test
    3.2 Preliminary leak testing
    3.3 Pressurization check
    3.4 Design limitations
    3.5 Equipment and setup

4.0 Safety Devices
    4.1 Pressure control valves and regulators
    4.2 Pressure relief valves and vents
    4.3 Flow rate of regulator and relief valves

5.0 Hazardous and Tracer Gas Safety
    5.1 Combustible gas detection and safety
    5.2 Toxic gas detection and safety
    5.3 Oxygen-deficiency detectors
    5.4 Radioisotope detection

6.0 Types of Monitoring Equipment
    6.1 Area monitors
    6.2 Personnel monitors
    6.3 Leak-locating devices

7.0 Safety Regulations
    7.1 State and federal regulations
    7.2 Safety codes/standards
    7.3 Hazardous gas standards
    7.4 Nuclear Regulatory Commission (NRC) radiation requirements

Leak Testing Methods Course

1.0 The following leak testing methods may be incorporated as applicable.
    1.1 Each of these methods can be further divided into major techniques as shown in the following examples.
        1.1.1 Bubble testing
            1.1.1.1 Immersion
            1.1.1.2 Film solution
        1.1.2 Ultrasonic testing
            1.1.2.1 Sonic/mechanical flow
            1.1.2.2 Sound generator
        1.1.3 Voltage discharge testing
            1.1.3.1 Voltage spark
            1.1.3.2 Color change
        1.1.4 Pressure leak testing
            1.1.4.1 Hydrostatic
            1.1.4.2 Pneumatic
        1.1.5 Ionization
            1.1.5.1 Photoionization
            1.1.5.2 Flame ionization
        1.1.6 Conductivity
            1.1.6.1 Thermal conductivity
            1.1.6.2 Solid state
        1.1.7 Radiation absorption
            1.1.7.1 Infrared
            1.1.7.2 Ultraviolet
            1.1.7.3 Laser
        1.1.8 Chemical-based
            1.1.8.1 Chemical penetrants
            1.1.8.2 Chemical gas tracer (colorimetric)

  1.1.9 Halogen detector
    1.1.9.1 Halide torch
    1.1.9.2 Electron capture
    1.1.9.3 Halogen diode
  1.1.10 Pressure change measurement
    1.1.10.1 Absolute
    1.1.10.2 Reference
    1.1.10.3 Pressure rise
    1.1.10.4 Flow
    1.1.10.5 Pressure decay
    1.1.10.6 Volumetric
  1.1.11 Mass spectrometer
    1.1.11.1 Helium or argon leak detector
    1.1.11.2 Residual gas analyzer
  1.1.12 Radioisotope

2.0 Leak Testing Method Course Outline
  2.1 The following may be applied to any of the listed methods.
  2.2 Terminology
  2.3 Basic techniques and/or units
    2.3.1 Leak location – measurement/monitoring
    2.3.2 Visual and other sensing devices
    2.3.3 Various techniques
  2.4 Testing materials and equipment
    2.4.1 Materials, gases/fluids used
    2.4.2 Control devices and operation
    2.4.3 Instrument/gages used
    2.4.4 Range and calibration of instrument/gages
  2.5 Testing principles and practices
    2.5.1 Pressure/vacuum and control used
    2.5.2 Principles of techniques used
    2.5.3 Effects of temperature and other atmospheric conditions
    2.5.4 Calibration for testing
    2.5.5 Probing/scanning or measurement/monitoring
    2.5.6 Leak interpretation evaluation
  2.6 Acceptance and rejection criteria
  2.7 Safety concerns
  2.8 Advantages and limitations
  2.9 Codes/standards

Leak Testing Level II Topical Outline

Principles of Leak Testing Course

1.0 Introduction
  1.1 Leak testing fundamentals
    1.1.1 Reasons for leak testing
    1.1.2 Functions of leak testing
    1.1.3 Terminology
    1.1.4 Leak testing units
    1.1.5 Leak conductance
  1.2 Leak testing standards
    1.2.1 Leak standards
    1.2.2 National Institute of Standards and Technology (NIST) traceability and calibration
    1.2.3 Instrument calibration versus test qualification
    1.2.4 System calibration techniques

Pressure and Vacuum Technology Course

Leak Test Selection Course

Leak Testing Level III Topical Outline

1.0 Principles/Theory
    1.1 Physical principles in leak testing
        1.1.1 Physical quantities
            1.1.1.1 Fundamental units
            1.1.1.2 Volume and pressure
            1.1.1.3 Time and temperature
            1.1.1.4 Absolute values
            1.1.1.5 Standard versus atmospheric conditions
            1.1.1.6 Leakage rates
        1.1.2 Structure of matter
            1.1.2.1 Atomic theory
            1.1.2.2 Ionization and ion pairs
            1.1.2.3 States of matter
            1.1.2.4 Molecular structure
            1.1.2.5 Diatomic and monatomic molecules
            1.1.2.6 Molecular weight
        1.1.3 Gas principles and law
            1.1.3.1 Brownian movement
            1.1.3.2 Mean free path
            1.1.3.3 Pressure and temperature effects on gases
            1.1.3.4 Pascal's law of pressure
            1.1.3.5 Charles' and Boyles' laws
            1.1.3.6 Ideal gas law
            1.1.3.7 Dalton's law of partial pressure
            1.1.3.8 Vapor pressure and effects in vacuum
        1.1.4 Gas properties
            1.1.4.1 Kinetic theory of gases
            1.1.4.2 Graham law of diffusion
            1.1.4.3 Stratification
            1.1.4.4 Avogadro's principle
            1.1.4.5 Gas law relationship
            1.1.4.6 General ideal gas law
            1.1.4.7 Gas mixture and concentration
            1.1.4.8 Gas velocity, density and viscosity
    1.2 Principles of gas flow
        1.2.1 Standard leaks
            1.2.1.1 Capillary
            1.2.1.2 Permeation
        1.2.2 Modes of gas flow
            1.2.2.1 Molecular and viscous
            1.2.2.2 Transitional
            1.2.2.3 Laminar, turbulent, sonic
        1.2.3 Factors affecting gas flow
        1.2.4 Geometry of leakage path
            1.2.4.1 Mean free flow of fluid
            1.2.4.2 Clogging and check valve effects
            1.2.4.3 Irregular aperture size
            1.2.4.4 Leak rate versus viscosity
            1.2.4.5 Temperature and atmospheric conditions
            1.2.4.6 Velocity gradient versus viscosity
            1.2.4.7 Reynolds number versus Knudsen number
        1.2.5 Principles of mass spectrometer testing
            1.2.5.1 Vacuum and pressure technology
            1.2.5.2 Outgassing of materials versus pressure
            1.2.5.3 Vacuum pumping technology

1.3   Proper selection of leak testing as method of choice
       1.3.1   Differences between leak testing and other methods
       1.3.2   Complementary roles of leak testing and other methods
       1.3.3   Potential for conflicting results between methods
       1.3.4   Factors that quality/disqualify the use of leak testing

2.0   Equipment/Material
    2.1   Leak testing standards
       2.1.1   Capillary or permeation
       2.1.2   National Institute of Standards and Technology (NIST) standards
       2.1.3   System versus instrument calibration
       2.1.4   Inaccuracy of calibration
    2.2   Detector/instrument performance factors
       2.2.1   Design and use
       2.2.2   Accuracy and precision
       2.2.3   Linearity (straight/logarithmic scale)
       2.2.4   Calibration and frequency
       2.2.5   Response and recovery time
    2.3   Vacuum pumps
       2.3.1   Mechanical pumps (positive displacement)
            2.3.1.1   Oil-sealed rotary pumps
                 2.3.1.1.1   Construction
                 2.3.1.1.2   Operation
                 2.3.1.1.3   Pump fluid
                 2.3.1.1.4   Difficulties with rotary pumps
                 2.3.1.1.5   Care of rotary pumps
            2.3.1.2   Vapor (diffusion) pumps
                 2.3.1.2.1   Construction
                 2.3.1.2.2   Operation
                 2.3.1.2.3   Pump fluid
                 2.3.1.2.4   Diagnosis of diffusion pump troubles
            2.3.1.3   Sublimation pumps (getter pumps)
            2.3.1.4   Ion pumps
            2.3.1.5   Turbomolecular pumps
            2.3.1.6   Absorption pumps
            2.3.1.7   Cryopumps
    2.4   Bubble testing practices and techniques
       2.4.1   Solutions
       2.4.2   Solution applicators
       2.4.3   Vacuum boxes
    2.5   Absolute pressure testing equipment
       2.5.1   Pressure measuring instruments
       2.5.2   Temperature measuring instruments
       2.5.3   Dew point measuring instruments
       2.5.4   Accuracy of equipment
       2.5.5   Calibration of equipment
       2.5.6   Reference panel instruments
       2.5.7   Reference system installation and testing
    2.6   Absolute pressure hold testing of containers
       2.6.1   Equation for determining pressure change
       2.6.2   Temperature measuring
    2.7   Absolute pressure leakage rate testing of containers
       2.7.1   Equation(s) for determining percent loss
       2.7.2   Positioning of temperature and dew point sensors for mean sampling accuracy
       2.7.3   Analysis of temperature and dew point data
    2.8   Analysis of data for determination of accurate results
    2.9   Halogen testing equipment
       2.9.1   Leak detector control unit
       2.9.2   Gun detectors

6.4 Safety devices
    6.4.1 Pressure control valves and regulators
    6.4.2 Pressure relief valves and vents
    6.4.3 Flow rate of regulator and relief valves
6.5 Hazardous and tracer gas safety
    6.5.1 Combustible gas detection and safety
    6.5.2 Toxic gas detection and safety
    6.5.3 Oxygen-deficiency detectors
    6.5.4 Radioisotope detection
6.6 Types of monitoring equipment
    6.6.1 Area monitors
    6.6.2 Personnel monitors
    6.6.3 Leak-locating devices
6.7 Safety
    6.7.1 State and federal regulations
    6.7.2 Safety codes/standards
    6.7.3 Hazardous gas standards
    6.7.4 Nuclear Regulatory Commission (NRC) radiation requirements

Training References
Leak Testing Method, Level I, II and III

ASNT Level III Study Guide: Leak Testing Method, Columbus, OH: The American Society for Nondestructive Testing, Inc. Latest edition.*

Annual Book of ASTM Standards, Vol. 03.03. Philadelphia, PA: American Society for Testing and Materials. Latest edition.*

ASME Boiler and Pressure Vessel Inspection Code B, Section V, Article 10, *Leak Testing.* New York: American Society of Mechanical Engineers. Latest edition.

Containment System Leakage Testing Requirements (ANSI/ANS 56.8). LaGrange Park, IL: American Nuclear Society. 1981.

Jackson, C.N. and C.N. Sherlock, technical eds., P.O. Moore, ed. *Nondestructive Testing Handbook*, third edition: Volume 1, *Leak Testing.* Columbus OH: The American Society for Nondestructive Testing, Inc. 1998.*

Mix, P.E. *Introduction to Nondestructive Testing: A Training Guide*, second edition. New York: John Wiley & Sons, Inc. 2005.

Nondestructive Evaluation and Quality Control: ASM Handbook, Volume 17. Metals Park, OH: ASM International. 1989.*

Supplement to Recommended Practice No. SNT-TC-1A (Q&A Book): Bubble Leak Testing. Columbus, OH: American Society for Nondestructive Testing, Inc. Latest edition.*

Supplement to Recommended Practice No. SNT-TC-1A (Q&A Book): Halogen Diode Detector. Columbus, OH: American Society for Nondestructive Testing, Inc. Latest edition.*

Supplement to Recommended Practice No. SNT-TC-1A (Q&A Book): Mass Spectrometer Testing Method. Columbus, OH: American Society for Nondestructive Testing, Inc. Latest edition.*

Supplement to Recommended Practice No. SNT-TC-1A (Q&A Book): Pressure Change Measurement Testing. Columbus, OH: American Society for Nondestructive Testing, Inc. Latest edition.*

Wilson, N. and L. Beavis. *Handbook of Vacuum Leak Detection.* New York: American Vacuum Society. 1988.

*   Available from The American Society for Nondestructive Testing, Inc., Columbus OH.

Liquid Penetrant Testing Level I Topical Outline

1.0 Introduction
    1.1 Brief history of nondestructive testing and liquid penetrant testing
    1.2 Purpose of liquid penetrant testing
    1.3 Basic principles of liquid penetrant testing
    1.4 Types of liquid penetrants commercially available
    1.5 Method of personnel qualification

2.0 Liquid Penetrant Processing
    2.1 Preparation of parts
    2.2 Adequate lighting
    2.3 Application of penetrant to parts
    2.4 Removal of surface penetrant
    2.5 Developer application and drying
    2.6 Inspection and evaluation
    2.7 Postcleaning

3.0 Various Penetrant Testing Methods
    3.1 Current ASTM and ASME standard methods – ASTM E 165, E 1208, E 1209, E 1210 and E 1417.
    3.2 Characteristics of each method
    3.3 General applications of each method

4.0 Liquid Penetrant Testing Equipment
    4.1 Liquid penetrant testing units
    4.2 Lighting for liquid penetrant testing equipment and light meters
    4.3 Materials for liquid penetrant testing
    4.4 Precautions in liquid penetrant inspection

Liquid Penetrant Testing Level II Topical Outline

1.0 Review
    1.1 Basic principles
    1.2 Process of various methods
    1.3 Equipment

2.0 Selection of the Appropriate Penetrant Testing Method
    2.1 Advantages of various methods
    2.2 Disadvantages of various methods

3.0 Inspection and Evaluation of Indications
    3.1 General
        3.1.1 Discontinuities inherent in various materials
        3.1.2 Reason for indications
        3.1.3 Appearance of indications
        3.1.4 Time for indications to appear
        3.1.5 Persistence of indications
        3.1.6 Effects of temperature and lighting (white to UV)
        3.1.7 Effects of metal smearing operations (shot peening, machining, etc.)
        3.1.8 Preferred sequence for penetrant inspection
        3.1.9 Part preparation (precleaning, stripping, etc.)
    3.2 Factors affecting indications
        3.2.1 Pre-cleaning
        3.2.2 Penetrant used
        3.2.3 Prior processing
        3.2.4 Technique used

3.3 Indications from cracks
    3.3.1 Cracks occurring during solidification
    3.3.2 Cracks occurring during processing
    3.3.3 Cracks occurring during service
3.4 Indications from porosity
3.5 Indications from specific material forms
    3.5.1 Forgings
    3.5.2 Castings
    3.5.3 Plate
    3.5.4 Welds
    3.5.5 Extrusions
3.6 Evaluation of indications
    3.6.1 True indications
    3.6.2 False indications
    3.6.3 Relevant indications
    3.6.4 Nonrelevant indications
    3.6.5 Process control
        3.6.5.1 Controlling process variables
        3.6.5.2 Testing and maintenance materials

4.0 Inspection Procedures and Standards
    4.1 Inspection procedures (minimum requirements)
    4.2 Standards/codes
        4.2.1 Applicable methods/processes
        4.2.2 Acceptance criteria

5.0 Basic Methods of Instruction

Liquid Penetrant Testing Level III Topical Outline

1.0 Principles/Theory
    1.1 Principles of liquid penetrant process
        1.1.1 Process variables
        1.1.2 Effects of test object factors on process
    1.2 Theory
        1.2.1 Physics of how penetrants work
        1.2.2 Control and measurement of penetrant process variables
            1.2.2.1 Surface tension, viscosity and capillary entrapment
            1.2.2.2 Measurement of penetrability, washability and emulsification
            1.2.2.3 Contrast, brightness and fluorescence
            1.2.2.4 Contamination of materials
            1.2.2.5 Proper selection of penetrant levels for different testing (sensitivity)
    1.3 Proper selection of PT as method of choice
        1.3.1 Difference between liquid penetrant testing and other methods
        1.3.2 Complementary roles of liquid penetrant testing and other methods
        1.3.3 Potential for conflicting results between methods
        1.3.4 Factors that qualify/disqualify the use of liquid penetrant testing
        1.3.5 Selection of liquid penetrant testing technique
    1.4 Liquid penetrant processing
        1.4.1 Preparation of parts
        1.4.2 Applications of penetrants and emulsifiers to parts
        1.4.3 Removal of surface penetrants
        1.4.4 Developer application and drying
        1.4.5 Evaluation
        1.4.6 Post cleaning
        1.4.7 Precautions

2.0 Equipment/Materials
    2.1   Methods of measurement
    2.2   Lighting for liquid penetrant testing
        2.2.1   White light intensity
        2.2.2   Ultraviolet radiation intensity, warm-up time, etc.
        2.2.3   Physics and physiological differences
    2.3   Materials for liquid penetrant testing
        2.3.1   Solvent removable
        2.3.2   Water-washable
        2.3.3   Post emulsifiable
            2.3.3.1   Water base (hydrophilic)
            2.3.3.2   Oil base (lipophilic)
        2.3.4   Dual sensitivity
    2.4   Testing and maintenance of materials

3.0 Interpretation/Evaluation
    3.1   General
        3.1.1   Appearance of penetrant indications
        3.1.2   Persistence of indications
    3.2   Factors affecting indications
        3.2.1   Preferred sequence for penetrant inspection
        3.2.2   Part preparation (pre-cleaning, stripping, etc.)
        3.2.3   Environment (lighting, temperature, etc.)
        3.2.4   Effect of metal smearing operations (shot peening, machining, etc.)
    3.3   Indications from discontinuities
        3.3.1   Metallic materials
        3.3.2   Nonmetallic materials
    3.4   Relevant and nonrelevant indications
        3.4.1   True indications
        3.4.2   False indications

4.0 Procedures

5.0 Safety and Health
    5.1   Toxicity
    5.2   Flammability
    5.3   Precautions for ultraviolet radiation
    5.4   Material safety data sheets (MSDS)

Training References
Liquid Penetrant Testing, Level I, II and III

Annual Book of ASTM Standards, Vol. 03.03, Nondestructive Testing. Philadelphia, PA: American Society for Testing and Materials. Latest edition.*

ASNT Level II Study Guide: Liquid Penetrant Testing Method, second edition. Columbus, OH: The American Society for Nondestructive Testing, Inc. Latest edition.*

ASNT Level III Study Guide: Liquid Penetrant Testing Method. Columbus, OH: The American Society for Nondestructive Testing, Inc. Latest edition.*

Badger, D. *Liquid Penetrant Testing Classroom Training Book* (PTP Series). Columbus, OH: The American Society for Nondestructive Testing, Inc. 2005.*

Boisvert, B. *Principles and Applications of Liquid Penetrant Testing: A Classroom Training Text.* Columbus, OH: The American Society for Nondestructive Testing, Inc. 1993.*

Lovejoy, D. *Penetrant Testing: A Practical Guide.* New York: Chapman & Hall. 1991.

Mix, P.E. *Introduction to Nondestructive Testing: A Training Guide,* second edition. New York: John Wiley & Sons. 2005.

Nondestructive Evaluation and Quality Control: ASM Handbook, Volume 17. Metals Park, OH: ASM International. 1989.*

Standard Reference Photographs for Liquid Penetrant Inspection: Adjunct to ASTM E 433. Philadelphia, PA: ASTM. 1985.*

Supplement to Recommended Practice No. SNT-TC-1A (Q&A Book): Liquid Penetrant Testing Method. Columbus, OH: American Society for Nondestructive Testing, Inc. Latest edition.*

Tracy, N., tech. ed., P.O. Moore, ed. *Nondestructive Testing Handbook*, third edition: Volume 2, *Liquid Penetrant Testing*. Columbus, OH: The American Society for Nondestructive Testing, Inc. 1999*

Welding Handbook, Volume 1. Miami, FL: American Welding Society. Latest edition.*

* Available from the American Society for Nondestructive Testing, Inc. Columbus, OH.

Magnetic Particle Testing Level I Topical Outline

1.0   Principles of Magnets and Magnetic Fields
    1.1   Theory of magnetic fields
        1.1.1   Earth's magnetic field
        1.1.2   Magnetic fields around magnetized materials
    1.2   Theory of magnetism
        1.2.1   Magnetic poles
        1.2.2   Law of magnetism
        1.2.3   Materials influenced by magnetic fields
            1.2.3.1   Ferromagnetic
            1.2.3.2   Paramagnetic
        1.2.4   Magnetic characteristics of nonferrous materials
    1.3   Terminology associated with magnetic particle testing

2.0   Characteristics of Magnetic Fields
    2.1   Bar magnet
    2.2   Ring magnet

3.0   Effect of Discontinuities of Materials
    3.1   Surface cracks
    3.2   Scratches
    3.3   Subsurface defects

4.0   Magnetization by Means of Electric Current
    4.1   Circular field
        4.1.1   Field around a straight conductor
        4.1.2   Right-hand rule
        4.1.3   Field in parts through which current flows
            4.1.3.1   Long, solid, cylindrical, regular parts
            4.1.3.2   Irregularly shaped parts
            4.1.3.3   Tubular parts
            4.1.3.4   Parts containing machined holes, slots, etc.
        4.1.4   Methods of inducing current flow in parts
            4.1.4.1   Contact plates
            4.1.4.2   Prods
        4.1.5   Discontinuities commonly discovered by circular fields
    4.2   Longitudinal field
        4.2.1   Field produced by current flow in a coil
        4.2.2   Field direction in a current-carrying coil
        4.2.3   Field strength in a current-carrying coil
        4.2.4   Discontinuities commonly discovered by longitudinal fields

Magnetic Particle Testing Level II Topical Outline

1.0 Principles
    1.1 Theory
        1.1.1 Flux patterns
        1.1.2 Frequency and voltage factors
        1.1.3 Current calculations
        1.1.4 Surface flux strength
        1.1.5 Subsurface effects
    1.2 Magnets and magnetism
        1.2.1 Distance factors versus strength of flux
        1.2.2 Internal and external flux patterns
        1.2.3 Phenomenon action at the discontinuity
        1.2.4 Heat effects on magnetism
        1.2.5 Material hardness versus magnetic retention

2.0 Flux Fields
    2.1 Direct current
        2.1.1 Depth of penetration factors
        2.1.2 Source of current
    2.2 Direct pulsating current
        2.2.1 Similarity to direct current
        2.2.2 Advantages
        2.2.3 Typical fields
    2.3 Alternating current
        2.3.1 Cyclic effects
        2.3.2 Surface strength characteristics
        2.3.3 Safety precautions
        2.3.4 Voltage and current factors
        2.3.5 Source of current

3.0 Effects of Discontinuities on Materials
    3.1 Design factors
        3.1.1 Mechanical properties
        3.1.2 Part use
    3.2 Relationship to load-carrying ability

4.0 Magnetization by Means of Electric Current
    4.1 Circular techniques
        4.1.1 Current calculations
        4.1.2 Depth-factor considerations
        4.1.3 Precautions – safety and overheating
        4.1.4 Contact prods and yokes
            4.1.4.1 Requirements for prods and yokes
            4.1.4.2 Current-carrying capabilities
        4.1.5 Discontinuities commonly detected
    4.2 Longitudinal technique
        4.2.1 Principles of induced flux fields
        4.2.2 Geometry of part to be inspected
        4.2.3 Shapes and sizes of coils
        4.2.4 Use of coils and cables
            4.2.4.1 Strength of field
            4.2.4.2 Current directional flow versus flux field
            4.2.4.3 Shapes, sizes and current capacities
        4.2.5 Current calculations
            4.2.5.1 Formulas
            4.2.5.2 Types of current required
            4.2.5.3 Current demand
        4.2.6 Discontinuities commonly detected

5.0 Selecting the Proper Method of Magnetization
   5.1 Alloy, shape and condition of part
   5.2 Type of magnetizing current
   5.3 Direction of magnetic field
   5.4 Sequence of operations
   5.5 Value of flux density

6.0 Demagnetization Procedures
   6.1 Need for demagnetization of parts
   6.2 Current, frequency and field orientation
   6.3 Heat factors and precautions
   6.4 Need for collapsing flux fields

7.0 Equipment
   7.1 Portable type
      7.1.1 Reason for portable equipment
      7.1.2 Capabilities of portable equipment
      7.1.3 Similarity to stationary equipment
   7.2 Stationary type
      7.2.1 Capability of handling large and heavy parts
      7.2.2 Flexibility in use
      7.2.3 Need for stationary equipment
      7.2.4 Use of accessories and attachments
   7.3 Automatic type
      7.3.1 Requirements for automation
      7.3.2 Sequential operations
      7.3.3 Control and operation factors
      7.3.4 Alarm and rejection mechanisms
   7.4 Multidirectional units
      7.4.1 Capability
      7.4.2 Control and operation factors
      7.4.3 Applications
   7.5 Liquids and powders
      7.5.1 Liquid requirements as a particle vehicle
      7.5.2 Safety precautions
      7.5.3 Temperature needs
      7.5.4 Powder and paste contents
      7.5.5 Mixing procedures
      7.5.6 Need for accurate proportions
   7.6 Ultraviolet radiation type
      7.6.1 Ultraviolet radiation and fluorescence
      7.6.2 Visible light and black light comparisons
      7.6.3 Requirements in the testing cycle
      7.6.4 Techniques in use
   7.7 Light-sensitive instruments
      7.7.1 Need for instrumentation
      7.7.2 Light characteristics

8.0 Types of Discontinuities
   8.1 In castings
   8.2 In ingots
   8.3 In wrought sections and parts
   8.4 In welds

9.0 Evaluation Techniques
   9.1 Use of standards – e.g. ASTM E 1444, E 709
      9.1.1 Need for standards and references
      9.1.2 Comparison of known with unknown
      9.1.3 Specifications and certifications
      9.1.4 Comparison techniques

9.2   Defect appraisal
    9.2.1   History of part
    9.2.2   Manufacturing process
    9.2.3   Possible causes of defect
    9.2.4   Use of part
    9.2.5   Acceptance and rejection criteria
    9.2.6   Use of tolerances

10.0   Quality Control of Equipment and Processes
    10.1   Malfunctioning of equipment
    10.2   Proper magnetic particles and bath liquid
    10.3   Bath concentration
        10.3.1   Settling test
        10.3.2   Other bath-strength tests
    10.4   Tests for ultraviolet radiation intensity

Magnetic Particle Testing Level III Topical Outline

1.0   Principles/Theory
    1.1   Principles of magnets and magnetic fields
        1.1.1   Theory of magnetic fields
        1.1.2   Theory of magnetism
        1.1.3   Terminology associated with magnetic particle testing
    1.2   Characteristics of magnetic fields
        1.2.1   Bar magnet
        1.2.2   Ring magnet

2.0   Equipment/Materials
    2.1   Magnetic particle test equipment
        2.1.1   Equipment selection considerations
        2.1.2   Manual inspection equipment
        2.1.3   Medium- and heavy-duty equipment
        2.1.4   Stationary equipment
        2.1.5   Mechanized inspection equipment
    2.2   Inspection materials
        2.2.1   Wet particle technique
        2.2.2   Dry particle technique

3.0   Technique/Calibrations
    3.1   Magnetization by means of electric current
        3.1.1   Circular field
            3.1.1.1   Field around a straight conductor
            3.1.1.2   Right-hand rule
            3.1.1.3   Field in parts through which current flows
            3.1.1.4   Methods of inducing current flow in parts
            3.1.1.5   Discontinuities commonly indicated by circular field
            3.1.1.6   Applications of circular magnetization
        3.1.2   Longitudinal field
            3.1.2.1   Field direction
            3.1.2.2   Discontinuities commonly indicated by longitudinal techniques
            3.1.2.3   Applications of longitudinal magnetization
    3.2   Selecting the proper method of magnetization
        3.2.1   Alloy, shape and condition of part
        3.2.2   Type of magnetizing field
        3.2.3   Direction of magnetic field
        3.2.4   Sequence of operation
        3.2.5   Value of flux density

3.3 Demagnetization
    3.3.1 Reasons for requiring demagnetization
    3.3.2 Methods of demagnetization

4.0 Interpretation/Evaluation
    4.1 Magnetic particle test indications and interpretations
    4.2 Effects of discontinuities on materials and types of discontinuities indicated by magnetic particle testing

5.0 Procedures
    5.1 Magnetic particle procedures, codes, standards and specifications

6.0 Safety and Health
    6.1 Precautions for ultraviolet radiation

Training References
Magnetic Particle Testing, Level I, II and III

Annual Book of ASTM Standards, Vol. 03.03, *Nondestructive Testing*. Philadelphia, PA: American Society for Testing and Materials. Latest edition.*

ASNT Level II Study Guide: Magnetic Particle Testing Method. Columbus, OH: The American Society for Nondestructive Testing, Inc. Latest edition.*

ASNT Level III Study Guide: Magnetic Particle Testing Method. Columbus, OH: The American Society for Nondestructive Testing, Inc. Latest edition.*

Betz, C.E. *Principles of Magnetic Particle Testing*. Chicago, IL: Magnaflux Corp. 2000.*

Mix, P.E., *Introduction to Nondestructive Testing: A Training Guide*, second edition. New York: John Wiley & Sons. 2005.

Moore, D.G., tech. ed., P.O. Moore, ed. *Nondestructive Testing Handbook*, third edition: Volume 8, *Magnetic Particle Testing*. Columbus, OH: The American Society for Nondestructive Testing, Inc. 2008.*

Nondestructive Evaluation and Quality Control: ASM Handbook, Volume 17. Metals Park, OH: ASM International. 1989.*

Smith, G. *Magnetic Particle Testing Classroom Training Book* (PTP Series). Columbus, OH: The American Society for Nondestructive Testing, Inc. 2004.*

Supplement to Recommended Practice No. SNT-TC-1A (Q&A Book): Magnetic Particle Method. Columbus, OH: The American Society for Nondestructive Testing, Inc. Latest edition.*

Welding Handbook, Volume 1. Miami, FL: American Welding Society. Latest edition.*

*   Available from the American Society for Nondestructive Testing, Inc., Columbus, OH.

Magnetic Flux Leakage Testing Level I Topical Outline

1.0 Magnetic Flux Leakage Testing
    1.1 Brief history of testing
    1.2 Basic principles of testing

2.0 Principles of Magnetic Fields
    2.1 Magnetic fields characteristics
    2.2 Flux line characteristics

3.0 Magnetism by Means of Electric Current

3.1 Field around a conductor
3.2 Right-hand rule
3.3 Field in ferromagnetic conductors

4.0 Indirect Magnetization
   4.1 Circular fields
   4.2 Longitudinal fields
   4.3 Transverse fields

5.0 Magnetization Variables
   5.1 Type of magnetizing current
   5.2 Alloy magnetic properties
      5.2.1 Hysteresis curve
      5.2.2 Permeability
      5.2.3 Factors affecting permeability

6.0 Flux Leakage
   6.1 Flux leakage theory
   6.2 Normal component of flux leakage

7.0 Search Coils
   7.1 Rate of change in the normal component of flux leakage
   7.2 Faraday's law (rate of change versus induced voltage)
   7.3 Factors that affect the voltage induced in a search coil

8.0 Hall Effect Search Units
   8.1 Hall effect principles
   8.2 Factors that affect the output voltage of Hall effect element

9.0 Signal Processing
   9.1 Rectification
   9.2 Filtering

10.0 Readout Mechanism
   10.1 Displays
   10.2 Strip-chart recorder
   10.3 Computerized data acquisition

Magnetic Flux Leakage Testing Level II Topical Outline

Magnetic Flux Leakage Evaluation Course

1.0 Review of Magnetic Theory
   1.1 Flux leakage theory
   1.2 Types of flux leakage sensing probes

2.0 Factors that Affect Flux Leakage Fields
   2.1 Degree of magnetization
   2.2 Defect geometry
   2.3 Defect location
   2.4 Defect orientation
   2.5 Distance between adjacent defects

3.0 Signal-to-Noise Ratio
   3.1 Definition
   3.2 Relationship to flux leakage testing
   3.3 Methods of improving signal-to-noise ratio

4.0 Selection of Method of Magnetization for Flux Leakage Testing
    4.1 Magnetization characteristics for various magnetic materials
    4.2 Magnetization by means of electric fields
        4.2.1 Circular field
        4.2.2 Longitudinal field
        4.2.3 Value of flux density
    4.3 Magnetization by means of permanent magnets
        4.3.1 Permanent magnet relationship and theory
        4.3.2 Permanent magnet materials
    4.4 Selection of proper magnetization method

5.0 Coupling
    5.1 "Lift-off" in flux leakage testing

6.0 Signal Processing Considerations
    6.1 Amplification
    6.2 Filtering

7.0 Applications
    7.1 General
        7.1.1 Flaw detection
        7.1.2 Sorting for properties related to permeability
        7.1.3 Measurement of magnetic-characteristic values
    7.2 Specific
        7.2.1 Tank floor and side inspection
        7.2.2 Wire rope inspection
        7.2.3 Tube inspection
        7.2.4 "Intelligent" pigs
        7.2.5 Bar inspection

8.0 User Standards and Operating Procedures
    8.1 Explanation of standards and specifications used in magnetic flux leakage testing
    8.2 Explanation of operating procedures used in magnetic flux leakage testing

Magnetic Flux Leakage Testing Level III Topical Outline

1.0 Principles/Theory
    1.1 Flux leakage theory
    1.2 Förster and other theories
    1.3 Finite element methods
    1.4 DC flux leakage/AC flux leakage

2.0 Equipment/Materials
    2.1 Detectors
        2.1.1 Advantages/limitations
    2.2 Coils
        2.2.1 Advantages/limitations
    2.3 Factors affecting choice of sensing elements
        2.3.1 Type of part to be inspected
        2.3.2 Type of discontinuity to be detected
        2.3.3 Speed of testing required
        2.3.4 Amount of testing required
        2.3.5 Probable location of discontinuity
        2.3.6 Applications other than discontinuity detection
    2.4 Read out selection
        2.4.1 Oscilloscope and other monitor displays
        2.4.2 Alarm, lights, etc.
        2.4.3 Marking system

Training References
Magnetic Flux Leakage Testing Method, Level I, II and III

Beissner, R.E., G.A. Matzkanin and C.M. Teller. NTIAC-80-1, *NDE Applications of Magnetic Leakage Field Methods*. January 1980.

Bray, D.E. and R.K. Stanley. *Nondestructive Evaluation, A Tool in Design, Manufacturing and Service*, revised edition. CRC Press. 1996.

MFL Compendium: Articles on Magnetic Flux Leakage – Collected from Materials Evaluation Published from 1953 to 2006. Columbus, OH: The American Society for Nondestructive Testing, Inc. 2010.*

Moore, D.G., tech. ed., P.O. Moore, ed. *Nondestructive Testing Handbook*, third edition: Volume 8, *Magnetic Particle Testing*. Columbus, OH: The American Society for Nondestructive Testing, Inc. 2008.*

Nondestructive Evaluation and Quality Control: ASM Handbook, Volume 17. Metals Park, OH: ASM International. 1989.*

Supplement to Recommended Practice No. SNT-TC-1A (Q&A Book): Electromagnetic Testing Method. Columbus, OH: The American Society for Nondestructive Testing, Inc. Latest edition.*

Udpa, S.S., tech. ed, P.O. Moore, ed. *Nondestructive Testing Handbook*, third edition: Volume 5, *Electromagnetic Testing*. Columbus, OH: American Society for Nondestructive Testing, Inc. 2004.*

*   Available from The American Society for Nondestructive Testing, Inc., Columbus OH.

Neutron Radiographic Testing Level I Topical Outline

Note: It is expected that the trainee receive 40 hours of radiation safety training instruction prior to performing work in radiography. The safety training does not count toward Level I or Level II training requirements. Basic radiation safety training should follow current government regulations. A Radiation Safety Topical Outline is available in Appendix A and can be used as guidance.

Basic Neutron Radiographic Physics Course

1.0   Introduction
-      1.1   History of industrial neutron radiography
-      1.2   General principles of examination of materials by penetrating radiation
-      1.3   Relationship of penetrating neutron radiation, radiography and radiometry
-      1.4   Comparison with other NDT methods, particularly with X-rays and gamma rays
-      1.5   General areas of application
  -          1.5.1   Imaging
  -          1.5.2   Metrology
  -          1.5.3   Product

2.0   Physical Principles
-      2.1   Sources for neutron radiography (general description)
  -          2.1.1   Isotopes
  -          2.1.2   Nuclear reactors
  -          2.1.3   Accelerators
-      2.2   Interaction between neutrons and matter
  -          2.2.1   Absorption
    -              2.2.1.1   Thermal neutrons
    -              2.2.1.2   Resonance neutrons
    -              2.2.1.3   Fast neutrons
  -          2.2.2   Scatter
    -              2.2.2.1   Elastic
    -              2.2.2.2   Inelastic
-      2.3   Neutron radiography techniques
  -          2.3.1   Film imaging techniques
  -          2.3.2   Nonfilm imaging techniques
-      2.4   Glossary of terms and units of measure

3.0   Radiation Sources for Neutrons (Specific Description)
-      3.1   Reactors
  -          3.1.1   Principle of fission chain reactions
  -          3.1.2   Neutron thermalization (slowing down)
  -          3.1.3   Thermal neutron flux
-      3.2   Accelerators
  -          3.2.1   Types of accelerators
  -          3.2.2   Neutron-producing reactions
-      3.3   Isotopic sources
  -          3.3.1   Radioisotope + Be

                3.3.1.1   α – Be
                3.3.1.2   Y – Be
        3.3.2   Radioisotope + D
                3.3.2.1   Y – D
        3.3.3   Spontaneous fission
                3.3.3.1 ^{252}Cf

4.0   Personnel Safety and Radiation Protection Review
    4.1   Hazards of excessive exposure
        4.1.1   General – beta-, gamma-radiation
        4.1.2   Specific neutron hazards
                4.1.2.1   Relative biological effectiveness
                4.1.2.2   Neutron activation
    4.2   Methods of controlling radiation dose
        4.2.1   Time
        4.2.2   Distance
        4.2.3   Shielding
    4.3   Specific equipment requirements
        4.3.1   Neutron monitoring dosimeters
        4.3.2   Gamma-ray monitoring dosimeters
        4.3.3   Radiation survey equipment
                4.3.3.1   Beta/gamma
                4.3.3.2   Neutron
        4.3.4   Recording/record keeping
    4.4   Radiation work procedures
    4.5   Federal, state and local regulations

Basic Neutron Radiographic Technique Course

1.0   Radiation-Detection Imaging
    1.1   Converter screens
        1.1.1   Principles of operation
        1.1.2   Direct-imaging screens
        1.1.3   Transfer-imaging screens
    1.2   Film – principles, properties and uses with neutron converter screens
        1.2.1   Radiation response
        1.2.2   Vacuum/contact considerations
        1.2.3   Radiographic speed
        1.2.4   Radiographic contrast
    1.3   Track-etch
        1.3.1   Radiation response
        1.3.2   Vacuum/contact considerations
        1.3.3   Radiographic speed
        1.3.4   Radiographic contrast

2.0   Neutron Radiographic Process: Basic Imaging Considerations
    2.1   Definition of sensitivity (including image quality indicators)
    2.2   Contrast and definition
        2.2.1   Neutron energy and neutron screen relationship
        2.2.2   Effect of scattering in object
    2.3   Geometric principles
    2.4   Generation and control of scatter
    2.5   Choice of neutron source
    2.6   Choice of film
    2.7   Use of exposure curves
    2.8   Cause of correction of unsatisfactory radiographs
        2.8.1   High film density
        2.8.2   Low film density

      2.8.3   High contrast
      2.8.4   Low contrast
      2.8.5   Poor definition
      2.8.6   Excessive film fog
      2.8.7   Light leaks
      2.8.8   Artifacts
  2.9   Arithmetic of exposure

3.0   Test Result Interpretation
  3.1   Relationship between X-ray and n-ray
  3.2   Effects on measurement and interpretation of test
  3.3   Administrative control of test quality by interpreter
  3.4   Familiarization with image

Neutron Radiographic Testing Level II Topical Outline

Neutron Radiographic Physics Course

1.0   Introduction
  1.1   General principles of examination of materials by penetrating radiation
  1.2   Relationship of penetrating neutron radiation, radiography and radiometry
  1.3   Comparison with other methods, particularly with X-rays and gamma rays
  1.4   Specific areas of application in industry

2.0   Review of Physical Principles
  2.1   Nature of penetrating radiation (all types)
      2.1.1   Particles
      2.1.2   Wave properties
      2.1.3   Electromagnetic waves
      2.1.4   Fundamentals of radiation physics
      2.1.5   Sources of radiation
          2.1.5.1   Electronic sources
          2.1.5.2   Isotopic sources
          2.1.5.3   Nuclear reactors
          2.1.5.4   Accelerators
  2.2   Interaction between penetrating radiation and matter (neutron and gamma ray)
      2.2.1   Absorption
      2.2.2   Scatter
      2.2.3   Other interactions
  2.3   Glossary of terms and units of measure

3.0   Radiation Sources for Neutrons
  3.1   Neutron sources – general
      3.1.1   Reactors
          3.1.1.1   Principle of fission chain reactions
          3.1.1.2   Fast-neutron flux – energy and spatial distribution
          3.1.1.3   Neutron thermalization
          3.1.1.4   Thermal-neutron flux – energy and spatial distribution
      3.1.2   Accelerators
          3.1.2.1   Types of accelerators
          3.1.2.2   Neutron-producing reactions
          3.1.2.3   Available yields and energy spectra
      3.1.3   Isotopic sources
          3.1.3.1   Radioisotope + Be
          3.1.3.2   Radioisotope + D
          3.1.3.3   Spontaneous fission ^{252}Cf

3.1.4   Beam design
    3.1.4.1   Source placement
    3.1.4.2   Collimation
    3.1.4.3   Filtering
    3.1.4.4   Shielding

4.0   Radiation Detection
  4.1   Imaging
    4.1.1   Converter screens
      4.1.1.1   Principles of operations
      4.1.1.2   Types of screens
        4.1.1.2.1   Direct exposure
        4.1.1.2.2   Transfer exposure
        4.1.1.2.3   Track-etch process
        4.1.1.2.4   Spectral sensitivity (each process)
    4.1.2   Film – principles, properties, use with neutron converter screens
      4.1.2.1   Material examination
      4.1.2.2   Monitoring
    4.1.3   Fluoroscopy
      4.1.3.1   Fluorescent screen
      4.1.3.2   Image amplification
      4.1.3.3   Cine techniques
    4.1.4   Direct TV viewing
    4.1.5   Special instrumentation associated with above techniques
  4.2   Non-imaging devices
    4.2.1   Solid state
      4.2.1.1   Scintillometer
      4.2.1.2   Photo-resistive devices
      4.2.1.3   Other
    4.2.2   Gaseous
      4.2.2.1   Proportional counters
      4.2.2.2   Geiger counters
      4.2.2.3   Ionization chambers
      4.2.2.4   Other
    4.2.3   Neutron detectors
      4.2.3.1   Boron-based gas counters
      4.2.3.2   Fission counters
      4.2.3.3   Helium-3 detectors
      4.2.3.4   Lithium-based scintillator
      4.2.3.5   Instrumentation
        4.2.3.5.1   Rate meters
        4.2.3.5.2   Counters
        4.2.3.5.3   Amplifiers and preamplifiers
        4.2.3.5.4   Recording readouts
        4.2.3.5.5   Other

5.0   Radiological Safety Principles Review
  5.1   Controlling personnel exposure
  5.2   Time, distance, shielding concepts
  5.3   As low as reasonably achievable (ALARA) concept
  5.4   Radiation-detection equipment
  5.5   Exposure-device operating characteristics

Neutron Radiographic Technique Course

1.0   Neutron Radiographic Process
  1.1   Basic neutron-imaging considerations

2.2 Material considerations
 2.2.1 Metallurgy or other material consideration as it affects use of item and test results
 2.2.2 Materials-processing effects on use of item and test results
 2.2.3 Discontinuities – their causes and effects
 2.2.4 Radiographic appearance of discontinuities
2.3 Codes, standards, specifications and procedures
 2.3.1 Thermal neutron radiography
 2.3.2 Resonance neutron radiography
 2.3.3 Other applicable codes, etc.

Neutron Radiographic Testing Level III Topical Outline

1.0 Principles/Theory
 1.1 Nature of penetrating radiation
 1.2 Interaction between penetrating radiation and matter
 1.3 Neutron radiography
  1.3.1 Imaging by film
  1.3.2 Imaging by fluorescent materials
  1.3.3 Imaging by electronic devices
 1.4 Radiometry

2.0 Equipment/Materials
 2.1 Sources of neutrons
  2.1.1 Reactors
  2.1.2 Accelerators
  2.1.3 Isotopic sources
  2.1.4 Beam control factors
 2.2 Radiation detectors
  2.2.1 Imaging
   2.2.1.1 Converter screens
   2.2.1.2 Film principles, properties, use with neutron converter screens
   2.2.1.3 Fluoroscopy
   2.2.1.4 TV and optical systems
 2.3 Non-imaging devices
  2.3.1 Solid state detectors
  2.3.2 Gaseous ionization detectors
  2.3.3 Neutron detectors
  2.3.4 Instrumentation
  2.3.5 Gaging and control processes

3.0 Techniques/Calibrations
 3.1 Blocking and filtering
 3.2 Multi-film technique
 3.3 Enlargement and projection
 3.4 Stereoradiography
 3.5 Triangulation methods
 3.6 Autoradiography
 3.7 Flash radiography
 3.8 In-motion radiography
 3.9 Fluoroscopy
 3.10 Electron emission radiography
 3.11 Micro-radiography
 3.12 Laminography (tomography)
 3.13 Control of diffraction effects
 3.14 Panoramic exposures
 3.15 Gaging
 3.16 Real time imaging
 3.17 Image analysis techniques

4.0 Interpretation/Evaluation
    4.1 Radiographic interpretation
        4.1.1 Image-object relationships
        4.1.2 Material considerations
            4.1.2.1 Material processing as it affects use of item and test results
            4.1.2.2 Discontinuities, their cause and effects
            4.1.2.3 Radiographic appearance of discontinuities
        4.1.3 Codes, standards and specifications

5.0 Procedures
    5.1 The radiographic process
        5.1.1 Imaging considerations
            5.1.1.1 Sensitivity
            5.1.1.2 Contrast and definition
            5.1.1.3 Geometric factors
            5.1.1.4 Intensifying screens
            5.1.1.5 Scattered radiation
            5.1.1.6 Source factors
            5.1.1.7 Detection media
            5.1.1.8 Exposure curves
    5.2 Film processing
        5.2.1 Darkroom procedures
        5.2.2 Darkroom equipment and chemicals
        5.2.3 Film processing
    5.3 Viewing of radiographs
        5.3.1 Illuminator requirements
        5.3.2 Background lighting
        5.3.3 Optical aids
    5.4 Judging radiographic quality
        5.4.1 Density
        5.4.2 Contrast
        5.4.3 Definition
        5.4.4 Artifacts
        5.4.5 Image quality indicators (IQIs)
        5.4.6 Causes and corrections of unsatisfactory radiographs

6.0 Safety and Health
    6.1 Personnel safety and radiation hazards
        6.1.1 Exposure hazards
            6.1.1.1 General – beta, gamma
            6.1.1.2 Specific neutron hazards
        6.1.2 Methods of controlling radiation exposure
        6.1.3 Operation and emergency procedures

Training References
Neutron Radiographic Testing, Level I, II and III

Annual Book of ASTM Standards, Vol. 03.03, *Nondestructive Testing*. Philadelphia, PA: American Society for Testing and Materials. Latest edition.*

Berger, H. *Neutron Radiography*. Amsterdam, Netherlands: Elsevier Publishing Co. 1965.

Berger, H. *Neutron Radiography and Gaging – STP 586*. Philadelphia, PA: American Society for Testing and Materials. 1967.

Bossi, R.H., F.A. Iddings and G.C. Wheeler, tech. eds., P.O. Moore, ed., *Nondestructive Testing Handbook*, third edition: Volume 4, *Radiographic Testing*. Columbus, OH: The American Society for Nondestructive Testing, Inc. 2002.*

Code of Federal Regulations, Title 10: Part 0-5. Washington D.C.: U.S. Government Printing Office. 1993.

Code of Federal Regulations, Title 10: Part 20. Washington D.C.: U.S. Government Printing Office. 1996.

Domanus, J.C. *Collimators for Thermal Neutron Radiography, An Overview*. D. Reidel Publishing Co. 1987.

Horns, A.A. and D.R. Wyman. *Mathematics and Physics of Neutron Radiography*. Reidel Publishing Co. 1986.

Mix, P.E. *Introduction to Nondestructive Testing: A Training Guide*, second edition. New York: John Wiley & Sons. 2005.

Nondestructive Evaluation and Quality Control: ASM Handbook, Volume 17. Metals Park, OH: ASM International. 1989.*

Radiography in Modern Industry, www.kodak.com/eknec/documents/87/0900688a802b3c87/Radiography-in-Modern-Industry.pdf. Rochester, NY: Eastman Kodak Co. 1980.

Supplement to Recommended Practice No. SNT-TC-1A (Q&A Book): Neutron Radiographic Testing Method. Columbus, OH: The American Society for Nondestructive Testing, Inc. Latest edition.*

* Available from the American Society for Nondestructive Testing, Inc., Columbus, OH.

Radiographic Testing Level I Topical Outline

Note: It is expected that the trainee receive 40 hours of radiation safety training instruction prior to performing work in radiography. The safety training does not count toward Level I or Level II training requirements. Basic radiation safety training should follow current government regulations. A Radiation Safety Topical Outline is available in Appendix A and can be used as guidance.

Basic Radiology Physics Course

1.0   Introduction
    1.1   History and discovery of radioactive materials
    1.2   Definition of industrial radiography
    1.3   Radiation protection – why?
    1.4   Basic math review – exponents, square root, etc.

2.0   Fundamental Properties of Matter
    2.1   Elements and atoms
    2.2   Molecules and compounds
    2.3   Atomic particles – properties of protons, electrons and neutrons
    2.4   Atomic structure
    2.5   Atomic number and weight
    2.6   Isotope versus radioisotope

3.0   Radioactive Materials
    3.1   Production
        3.1.1   Neutron activation
        3.1.2   Nuclear fission
    3.2   Stable versus unstable (radioactive) atoms
    3.3   Becquerel – the unit of activity
    3.4   Half-life of radioactive materials
    3.5   Plotting of radioactive decay
    3.6   Specific activity – becquerels/gram

4.0   Types of Radiation
    4.1   Particulate radiation – properties: alpha, beta, neutron
    4.2   Electromagnetic radiation – X-ray, gamma ray
    4.3   X-ray production
    4.4   Gamma-ray production

*   Topics may be deleted if the employer does not use these methods and techniques.

Radiographic Technique Course

1.0 Introduction
  1.1 Process of radiography
  1.2 Types of electromagnetic radiation sources
  1.3 Electromagnetic spectrum
  1.4 Penetrating ability or "quality" of X-rays and gamma rays
  1.5 Spectrum of X-ray tube source
  1.6 Spectrum of gamma-radioisotope source
  1.7 X-ray tube – change of mA or kVp effect on "quality" and intensity

2.0 Basic Principles of Radiography
  2.1 Geometric exposure principles
    2.1.1 "Shadow" formation and distortion
    2.1.2 Shadow enlargement calculation
    2.1.3 Shadow sharpness
    2.1.4 Geometric unsharpness
    2.1.5 Finding discontinuity depth
  2.2 Radiographic screens
    2.2.1 Lead intensifying screens
    2.2.2 Fluorescent intensifying screens
    2.2.3 Intensifying factors
    2.2.4 Importance of screen-to-film contact
    2.2.5 Importance of screen cleanliness and care
    2.2.6 Techniques for cleaning screens
  2.3 Radiographic cassettes
  2.4 Composition of industrial radiographic film
  2.5 The "heel effect" with X-ray tubes

3.0 Radiographs
  3.1 Formation of the latent image on film
  3.2 Inherent unsharpness
  3.3 Arithmetic of radiographic exposure
    3.3.1 Milliamperage – distance-time relationship
    3.3.2 Reciprocity law
    3.3.3 Photographic density
    3.3.4 X-ray exposure charts – material thickness, kV and exposure
    3.3.5 Gamma-ray exposure chart
    3.3.6 Inverse square-law considerations
    3.3.7 Calculation of exposure time for gamma- and X-ray sources
  3.4 Characteristic (Hurter and Driffield) curve
  3.5 Film speed and class descriptions
  3.6 Selection of film for particular purpose

4.0 Radiographic Image Quality
  4.1 Radiographic sensitivity
  4.2 Radiographic contrast
  4.3 Film contrast
  4.4 Subject contrast
  4.5 Definition
  4.6 Film graininess and screen mottle effects
  4.7 Image quality indicators

5.0 Film Handling, Loading and Processing
  5.1 Safe light and darkroom practices
  5.2 Loading bench and cleanliness
  5.3 Opening of film boxes and packets
  5.4 Loading of film and sealing cassettes

5.5   Handling techniques for "green film"
5.6   Elements of manual film processing

6.0   Exposure Techniques – Radiography
      6.1   Single-wall radiography
      6.2   Double-wall radiography
          6.2.1   Viewing two walls simultaneously
          6.2.2   Offset double-wall exposure single-wall viewing
          6.2.3   Elliptical techniques
      6.3   Panoramic radiography
      6.4   Use of multiple-film loading
      6.5   Specimen configuration

7.0   Fluoroscopic Techniques
      7.1   Dark adaptation and eye sensitivity
      7.2   Special scattered radiation techniques
      7.3   Personnel protection
      7.4   Sensitivity
      7.5   Limitations
      7.6   Direct screen viewing
      7.7   Indirect and remote screen viewing

Radiographic Testing Level II Topical Outline

Film Quality and Manufacturing Processes Course

1.0   Review of Basic Radiographic Principles
      1.1   Interaction of radiation with matter
      1.2   Math review
      1.3   Exposure calculations
      1.4   Geometric exposure principles
      1.5   Radiographic-image quality parameters

2.0   Darkroom Facilities, Techniques and Processing
      2.1   Facilities and equipment
          2.1.1   Automatic film processor versus manual processing
          2.1.2   Safe lights
          2.1.3   Viewer lights
          2.1.4   Loading bench
          2.1.5   Miscellaneous equipment
      2.2   Film loading
          2.2.1   General rules for handling unprocessed film
          2.2.2   Types of film packaging
          2.2.3   Cassette-loading techniques for sheet and roll
      2.3   Protection of radiographic film in storage
      2.4   Processing of film – manual
          2.4.1   Developer and replenishment
          2.4.2   Stop bath
          2.4.3   Fixer and replenishment
          2.4.4   Washing
          2.4.5   Prevention of water spots
          2.4.6   Drying
      2.5   Automatic film processing
      2.6   Film filing and storage
          2.6.1   Retention-life measurements
          2.6.2   Long-term storage
          2.6.3   Filing and separation techniques

2.7   Unsatisfactory radiographs – causes and cures
    2.7.1   High film density
    2.7.2   Insufficient film density
    2.7.3   High contrast
    2.7.4   Low contrast
    2.7.5   Poor definition
    2.7.6   Fog
    2.7.7   Light leaks
    2.7.8   Artifacts

2.8   Film density
    2.8.1   Step-wedge comparison film
    2.8.2   Densitometers

3.0   Indications, Discontinuities and Defects
  3.1   Indications
  3.2   Discontinuities
    3.2.1   Inherent
    3.2.2   Processing
    3.2.3   Service
  3.3   Defects

4.0   Manufacturing Processes and Associated Discontinuities
  4.1   Casting processes and associated discontinuities
    4.1.1   Ingots, blooms and billets
    4.1.2   Sand casting
    4.1.3   Centrifugal casting
    4.1.4   Investment casting
  4.2   Wrought processes and associated discontinuities
    4.2.1   Forgings
    4.2.2   Rolled products
    4.2.3   Extruded products
  4.3   Welding processes and associated discontinuities
    4.3.1   Submerged arc welding (SAW)
    4.3.2   Shielded metal arc welding (SMAW)
    4.3.3   Gas metal arc welding (GMAW)
    4.3.4   Flux corded arc welding (FCAW)
    4.3.5   Gas tungsten arc welding (GTAW)
    4.3.6   Resistance welding
    4.3.7   Special welding processes – electron beam, electroslag, electrogas, etc.

5.0   Radiological Safety Principles Review
  5.1   Controlling personnel exposure
  5.2   Time, distance, shielding concepts
  5.3   As low as reasonably achievable (ALARA) concept
  5.4   Radiation-detection equipment
  5.5   Exposure-device operating characteristics

Radiographic Evaluation and Interpretation Course

1.0   Radiographic Viewing
  1.1   Film-illuminator requirements
  1.2   Background lighting
  1.3   Multiple-composite viewing
  1.4   Image quality indicator placement
  1.5   Personnel dark adaptation and visual acuity
  1.6   Film identification
  1.7   Location markers

1.8   Film-density measurement
1.9   Film artifacts

2.0   Application Techniques
    2.1   Multiple-film techniques
        2.1.1   Thickness-variation parameters
        2.1.2   Film speed
        2.1.3   Film latitude
    2.2   Enlargement and projection
    2.3   Geometrical relationships
        2.3.1   Geometrical unsharpness
        2.3.2   Image quality indicator sensitivity
        2.3.3   Source-to-film distance
        2.3.4   Focal-spot size
    2.4   Triangulation methods for discontinuity location
    2.5   Localized magnification
    2.6   Film-handling techniques

3.0   Evaluation of Castings
    3.1   Casting-method review
    3.2   Casting discontinuities
    3.3   Origin and typical orientation of discontinuities
    3.4   Radiographic appearance
    3.5   Casting codes/standards – applicable acceptance criteria
    3.6   Reference radiographs

4.0   Evaluation of Weldments
    4.1   Welding-method review
    4.2   Welding discontinuities
    4.3   Origin and typical orientation of discontinuities
    4.4   Radiographic appearance
    4.5   Welding codes/standards – applicable acceptance criteria
    4.6   Reference radiographs or pictograms

5.0   Standards, Codes and Procedures for Radiography
    5.1   ASTM standards
    5.2   Acceptable radiographic techniques and setups
    5.3   Applicable employer procedures
    5.4   Procedure for radiograph parameter verification
    5.5   Radiographic reports

Computed Radiography Testing Level I Topical Outline

Note: It is expected that the trainee receive 40 hours of radiation safety training instruction prior to performing work in radiography. The safety training does not count toward Level I or Level II training requirements. Basic radiation safety training should follow current government regulations. A Radiation Safety Topical Outline is available in Appendix A and can be used as guidance.

Basic Radiology Physics Course

1.0   Introduction
    1.1   History and discovery of radioactive materials
    1.2   Definition of industrial radiography
    1.3   Radiation protection – why?
    1.4   Basic math review: exponents, square root, etc.

2.0 Fundamental Properties of Matter
    2.1 Elements and atoms
    2.2 Molecules and compounds
    2.3 Atomic particles – properties of protons, electrons and neutrons
    2.4 Atomic structure
    2.5 Atomic number and weight
    2.6 Isotope versus radioisotope

3.0 Radioactive Materials
    3.1 Production
        3.1.1 Neutron activation
        3.1.2 Nuclear fission
    3.2 Stable versus unstable (radioactive) atoms
    3.3 Becquerel – the unit of activity
    3.4 Half-life of radioactive materials
    3.5 Plotting of radioactive decay
    3.6 Specific activity – becquerels/gram

4.0 Types of Radiation
    4.1 Particulate radiation – properties: alpha, beta, neutron
    4.2 Electromagnetic radiation – X-ray, gamma ray
    4.3 X-ray production
    4.4 Gamma-ray production
    4.5 Gamma-ray energy
    4.6 Energy characteristics of common radioisotope sources
    4.7 Energy characteristics of X-ray machines

5.0 Interaction of Radiation with Matter
    5.1 Ionization
    5.2 Radiation interaction with matter
        5.2.1 Photoelectric effect
        5.2.2 Compton scattering
        5.2.3 Pair production
    5.3 Unit of radiation exposure – coulomb per kilogram (C/kg)
    5.4 Emissivity of commonly used radiographic sources
    5.5 Emissivity of X-ray exposure devices
    5.6 Attenuation of electromagnetic radiation – shielding
    5.7 Half-value layers, tenth-value layers
    5.8 Inverse square law

6.0 Exposure Devices and Radiation Sources
    6.1 Radioisotope sources
        6.1.1 Sealed-source design and fabrication
        6.1.2 Gamma-ray sources
        6.1.3 Beta and bremsstrahlung sources
        6.1.4 Neutron sources
    6.2 Radioisotope exposure device characteristics
    6.3 Electronic radiation sources – 500 keV and less, low energy
        6.3.1 Generator – high-voltage rectifiers
        6.3.2 X-ray tube design and fabrication
        6.3.3 X-ray control circuits
        6.3.4 Accelerating potential
        6.3.5 Target material and configuration
        6.3.6 Heat dissipation
        6.3.7 Duty cycle
        6.3.8 Beam filtration
    6.4* Electronic radiation sources – medium- and high-energy
        6.4.1* Resonance transformer
        6.4.2* Van de graaff accelerator
        6.4.3* Linear accelerator

6.4.4* Betatron
6.4.5* Coulomb per kilogram (C/kg) output
6.4.6* Equipment design and fabrication
6.4.7* Beam filtration

7.0 Radiological Safety Principles Review
7.1 Controlling personnel exposure
7.2 Time, distance, shielding concepts
7.3 As low as reasonably achievable (ALARA) concept
7.4 Radiation-detection equipment
7.5 Exposure-device operating characteristics

* Topics may be deleted if the employer does not use these methods and techniques.

Computed Radiography Technique Course

1.0 Computed Radiology (CR) Overview
1.1 Photostimulable luminescence (PSL)
1.2 Comparison of film radiography and CR
1.3 Digital images
1.3.1 Bits
1.3.2 Bytes
1.3.3 Pixels/voxels
1.3.4 Image file formats and compression
1.4 Advantages
1.5 Disadvantages
1.6 Examples

2.0 System Components
2.1 Imaging plates (IP)
2.2 IP readout devices
2.3 Monitors
2.4 Computers

3.0 Basic CR Techniques
3.1 Image acquisition
3.2 Image quality indicators
3.3 Display of acquired images
3.4 Optimization of displayed image
3.5 Storage of acquired and optimized image

4.0 Digital Image Processing
4.1 Enhanced images
4.2 Signal-to-noise ratio (SNR)
4.3 Artifacts and anomalies

Computed Radiography Testing Level II Topical Outline

Advanced Computed Radiography Course

1.0 Computed Radiography (CR) Overview
1.1 Photostimulable luminescence (PSL)
1.2 Image acquisition
1.3 Image presentation
1.4 Artifacts

2.0 Image Display Characteristics
    2.1   Image definition
    2.2   Filtering techniques
    2.3   Signal-to-noise ratio (SNR)
    2.4   Modulation transfer function (MTF)
    2.5   Grayscale adjustments
    2.6   Image quality indicators

3.0 Image Viewing
    3.1   Image-monitor requirements
    3.2   Background lighting
    3.3   Image quality indicator (IQI) placement
    3.4   Personnel dark adaptation and visual acuity
    3.5   Image identification
    3.6   Location markers

4.0 Evaluation of CR Images
    4.1   Pixel value
    4.2   IQI
    4.3   Artifact mitigation
    4.4   System performance
    4.5   Conformance to specifications
    4.6   Image storage and transmission

5.0 Application Techniques
    5.1   Multiple-view techniques
        5.1.1   Thickness-variation parameters
    5.2   Enlargement and projection
    5.3   Geometric relationships
        5.3.1   Geometric unsharpness
        5.3.2   Image quality indicator sensitivity
        5.3.3   Source-to-image plate distance
        5.3.4   Focal-spot size
    5.4   Localized magnification
    5.5   Plate-handling techniques

6.0 Evaluation of Castings
    6.1   Casting-method review
    6.2   Casting discontinuities
    6.3   Origin and typical orientation of discontinuities
    6.4   Radiographic appearance
    6.5   Casting codes/standards – applicable acceptance criteria
    6.6   Reference radiographs or images

7.0 Evaluation of Weldments
    7.1   Welding-method review
    7.2   Welding discontinuities
    7.3   Origin and typical orientation of discontinuities
    7.5   Welding codes/standards – applicable acceptance criteria
    7.6   Reference radiographs or images

8.0 Standards, Codes and Procedures for Radiography
    8.1   ASTM/ASME standards
    8.2   Acceptable radiographic techniques and setups
    8.3   Applicable employer procedures

9.0 Radiological Safety Principles Review
    9.1   Controlling personnel exposure
    9.2   Time, distance, shielding concepts
    9.3   As low as reasonably achievable (ALARA) concept

Computed Tomography Testing Level I Topical Outline

Note: It is expected that the trainee receive 40 hours of radiation safety training instruction prior to performing work in radiography. The safety training does not count toward Level I or Level II training requirements. Basic radiation safety training should follow current government regulations. A Radiation Safety Topical Outline is available in Appendix A and can be used as guidance.

Basic Radiology Physics Course

1.0   Introduction
    1.1   History and discovery of radioactive materials
    1.2   Definition of industrial radiography
    1.3   Radiation protection – why?
    1.4   Basic math review: exponents, square root, etc.

2.0   Fundamental Properties of Matter
    2.1   Elements and atoms
    2.2   Molecules and compounds
    2.3   Atomic particles – properties of protons, electrons and neutrons
    2.4   Atomic structure
    2.5   Atomic number and weight
    2.6   Isotope versus radioisotope

3.0   Radioactive Materials
    3.1   Production
        3.1.1   Neutron activation
        3.1.2   Nuclear fission
    3.2   Stable versus unstable (radioactive) atoms
    3.3   Becquerel – the unit of activity
    3.4   Half-life of radioactive materials
    3.5   Plotting of radioactive decay
    3.6   Specific activity – becquerels/gram

4.0   Types of Radiation
    4.1   Particulate radiation – properties: alpha, beta, neutron
    4.2   Electromagnetic radiation – X-ray, gamma ray
    4.3   X-ray production
    4.4   Gamma-ray production
    4.5   Gamma-ray energy
    4.6   Energy characteristics of common radioisotope sources
    4.7   Energy characteristics of X-ray machines

5.0   Interaction of Radiation with Matter
    5.1   Ionization
    5.2   Radiation interaction with matter
        5.2.1   Photoelectric effect
        5.2.2   Compton scattering
        5.2.3   Pair production
    5.3   Unit of radiation exposure – coulomb per kilogram (C/kg)
    5.4   Emissivity of commonly used radiographic sources
    5.5   Emissivity of X-ray exposure devices
    5.6   Attenuation of electromagnetic radiation – shielding

5.7 Half-value layers, tenth-value layers

5.8 Inverse square law

6.0 Exposure Devices and Radiation Sources
    6.1 Radioisotope sources
        6.1.1 Sealed-source design and fabrication
        6.1.2 Gamma-ray sources
        6.1.3 Beta and bremsstrahlung sources
        6.1.4 Neutron sources
    6.2 Radioisotope exposure device characteristics
    6.3 Electronic radiation sources – 500 keV and less, low energy
        6.3.1 Generator – high-voltage rectifiers
        6.3.2 X-ray tube design and fabrication
        6.3.3 X-ray control circuits
        6.3.4 Accelerating potential
        6.3.5 Target material and configuration
        6.3.6 Heat dissipation
        6.3.7 Duty cycle
        6.3.8 Beam filtration
    6.4* Electronic radiation sources – medium- and high-energy
        6.4.1* Resonance transformer
        6.4.2* Van de graaff accelerator
        6.4.3* Linear accelerator
        6.4.4* Betatron
        6.4.5* Coulomb per kilogram (C/kg) output
        6.4.6* Equipment design and fabrication
        6.4.7* Beam filtration

7.0 Radiological Safety Principles Review
    7.1 Controlling personnel exposure
    7.2 Time, distance, shielding concepts
    7.3 As low as reasonably achievable (ALARA) concept
    7.4 Radiation-detection equipment
    7.5 Exposure-device operating characteristics

* Topics may be deleted if the employer does not use these methods and techniques.

Basic Computed Tomography Technique Course

1.0 Computed Tomography (CT) Overview
    1.1 Difference between CT and conventional radiography
    1.2 Benefits and advantages
    1.3 Limitations
    1.4 Industrial imaging examples

2.0 Basic Hardware Configuration
    2.1 Scan geometries – general configurations by generation
    2.2 Radiation sources
    2.3 Detection systems
    2.4 Manipulation/mechanical system
    2.5 Computer system
    2.6 Image reconstruction
    2.7 Image display
    2.8 Data storage
    2.9 Operator interface

3.0 Fundamental CT Performance Parameters
   3.1 Fundamental scan plan parameters
   3.2 Basic system tradeoffs for spatial resolution/noise/slice thickness

4.0 Basic Image Interpretation and Processing
   4.1 Artifacts – definitions, detection and basic causes
   4.2 CT density measurements

Computed Tomography Testing Level II Topical Outline

Computed Tomography Technique Course

1.0 General Principles of CT and Terminology
   1.1 CT technical background
   1.2 Physical basis – X-ray interactions with material properties
   1.3 Mathematical basis – line integrals
   1.4 Data sampling principles
   1.5 Physical limitations of the sampling process
   1.6 Reconstruction algorithms
      1.6.1 Convolution/backprojections
      1.6.2 Fourier reconstructions
      1.6.3 Fan/cone beam

2.0 CT System Performance – Characterizing System Performance
   2.1 CT system performance parameters overview
   2.2 Spatial resolution
   2.3 Contrast sensitivity
   2.4 Artifacts
      2.4.1 Beam hardening, streak, under-sampling, etc.
   2.5 Noise
   2.6 Effective X-ray energy
   2.7 System performance measurement techniques
   2.8 Spatial resolution
   2.9 Contrast sensitivity
      2.9.1 Calibrating CT density
      2.9.2 Measuring CT density
      2.9.3 Performance measurement intervals

3.0 Image Interpretation and Processing
   3.1 Use of phantoms to monitor CT system performance
   3.2 Evaluation of CT system performance parameters
   3.3 Determination of artifacts
   3.4 Artifact mitigation techniques

4.0 Advanced Image Processing Algorithms
   4.1 Modulation transfer function calculation
   4.2 Effective energy calculation
   4.3 Application of image processing algorithms
   4.4 Artifact mitigation techniques application

5.0 Radiological Safety Principles Review
   5.1 Controlling personnel exposure
   5.2 Time, distance, shielding concepts
   5.3 As low as reasonably achievable (ALARA) concept
   5.4 Radiation-detection equipment
   5.5 Exposure-device operating characteristics

Radiographic Evaluation and Interpretation Course

1.0   Evaluation of Castings
    1.1   Casting-method review
    1.2   Casting discontinuities
    1.3   Origin and typical orientation of discontinuities
    1.4   Radiographic appearance
    1.5   Casting codes/standards – applicable acceptance criteria

2.0   Evaluation of Weldments
    2.1   Welding-method review
    2.2   Welding discontinuities
    2.3   Origin and typical orientation of discontinuities
    2.4   Welding codes/standards – applicable acceptance criteria

3.0   Standards, Codes and Procedures for Radiography
    3.1   ASTM standards
    3.2   Acceptable radiographic techniques and setups
    3.3   Applicable employer procedures

Digital Radiography Testing Level I Topical Outline

Note: It is expected that the trainee receive 40 hours of radiation safety training instruction prior to performing work in radiography. The safety training does not count toward Level I or Level II training requirements. Basic radiation safety training should follow current government regulations. A Radiation Safety Topical Outline is available in Appendix A and can be used as guidance.

Basic Radiology Physics Course

1.0   Introduction
    1.1   History and discovery of radioactive materials
    1.2   Definition of industrial radiography
    1.3   Radiation protection – why?
    1.4   Basic math review: exponents, square root, etc.

2.0   Fundamental Properties of Matter
    2.1   Elements and atoms
    2.2   Molecules and compounds
    2.3   Atomic particles – properties of protons, electrons and neutrons
    2.4   Atomic structure
    2.5   Atomic number and weight
    2.6   Isotope versus radioisotope

3.0   Radioactive Materials
    3.1   Production
        3.1.1   Neutron activation
        3.1.2   Nuclear fission
    3.2   Stable versus unstable (radioactive) atoms
    3.3   Becquerel – the unit of activity
    3.4   Half-life of radioactive materials
    3.5   Plotting of radioactive decay
    3.6   Specific activity – becquerels/gram

4.0 Types of Radiation
    4.1   Particulate radiation – properties: alpha, beta, neutron
    4.2   Electromagnetic radiation – X-ray, gamma ray
    4.3   X-ray production
    4.4   Gamma-ray production
    4.5   Gamma-ray energy
    4.6   Energy characteristics of common radioisotope sources
    4.7   Energy characteristics of X-ray machines

5.0 Interaction of Radiation with Matter
    5.1   Ionization
    5.2   Radiation interaction with matter
        5.2.1   Photoelectric effect
        5.2.2   Compton scattering
        5.2.3   Pair production
    5.3   Unit of radiation exposure – coulomb per kilogram (C/kg)
    5.4   Emissivity of commonly used radiographic sources
    5.5   Emissivity of X-ray exposure devices
    5.6   Attenuation of electromagnetic radiation – shielding
    5.7   Half-value layers, tenth-value layers
    5.8   Inverse square law

6.0 Exposure Devices and Radiation Sources
    6.1   Radioisotope sources
        6.1.1   Sealed-source design and fabrication
        6.1.2   Gamma-ray sources
        6.1.3   Beta and bremsstrahlung sources
        6.1.4   Neutron sources
    6.2   Radioisotope exposure device characteristics
    6.3   Electronic radiation sources – 500 keV and less, low-energy
        6.3.1   Generator – high-voltage rectifiers
        6.3.2   X-ray tube design and fabrication
        6.3.3   X-ray control circuits
        6.3.4   Accelerating potential
        6.3.5   Target material and configuration
        6.3.6   Heat dissipation
        6.3.7   Duty cycle
        6.3.8   Beam filtration
    6.4*   Electronic radiation sources – medium- and high-energy
        6.4.1*   Resonance transformer
        6.4.2*   Van de graaff accelerator
        6.4.3*   Linear accelerator
        6.4.4*   Betatron
        6.4.5*   Coulomb per kilogram (C/kg) output
        6.4.6*   Equipment design and fabrication
        6.4.7*   Beam filtration

7.0 Radiological Safety Principles Review
    7.1   Controlling personnel exposure
    7.2   Time, distance, shielding concepts
    7.3   As low as reasonably achievable (ALARA) concept
    7.4   Radiation-detection equipment
    7.5   Exposure-device operating characteristics

*   Topics may be deleted if the employer does not use these methods and techniques.

Basic Digital Radiography Technique Course

1.0   Digital Radiography (DR) Overview
     1.1   Digital radiography
     1.2   Digital images
         1.2.1   Bits/bytes
         1.2.2   Pixels/voxels
     1.3   Image file formats and compression
     1.4   DR system overview
     1.5   DR system capabilities
         1.5.1   DR versus film procedural steps
         1.5.2   Cost and environmental issues

2.0   DR System Components
     2.1   Detector(s) used in the radiography shop
         2.1.1   Operating procedures to use the equipment

3.0   Image Fidelity Indicators (System Characterization)
     3.1   Image quality indicators (IQIs): hole and wire types
     3.2   Line pair gages
     3.3   Phantoms
     3.4   Reference quality indicators (RQIs)
     3.5   TV test patterns

4.0   Detector Issues
     4.1   Scatter sensitivity
     4.2   Radiation exposure tolerance
     4.3   Portability
     4.4   Detector handling

5.0   Technique Sheets

Digital Radiography Testing Level II Topical Outline

Digital Radiography Technique Course

1.0   Basic Digital Radiography versus Film Principles
     1.1   Film versus DR images
         1.1.1   Linearity and latitude
         1.1.2   Contrast and resolution

2.0   DR System Components
     2.1   X-ray and gamma-ray sources
         2.1.1   Energy, mA, focal spot
         2.1.2   Stability
         2.1.3   Open and closed X-ray tubes
         2.1.4   Filtration
     2.2   Computer
         2.2.1   Operator interface
         2.2.2   System controller
         2.2.3   Image processor
     2.3   Monitors
         2.3.1   CRT
         2.3.2   LCD

8.0 Technique Development Considerations
    8.1 Image unsharpness and geometric magnification
        8.1.1 Determining required geometric magnification
        8.1.2 Geometry and geometric unsharpness
        8.1.3 Focal spot size measurement method
        8.1.4 Total image unsharpness
    8.2 SNR compensation for spatial resolution
        8.2.1 Frame averaging
        8.2.2 Binning
        8.2.3 X-ray spectrum optimization
            8.2.3.1 Filtering
            8.2.3.2 Beam collimation
            8.2.3.3 Beam energy
    8.3 Image processing
        8.3.1 Understanding of cost and benefits of common image processing techniques – windowing, filtering, subtraction, etc.

9.0 Detector Monitoring

10.0 Detector Maintenance

11.0 Use of Digital Reference Images
    11.1 ASTM standards review
    11.2 Use of reference images and contrast normalization

12.0 Radiological Safety Principles Review
    12.1 Controlling personnel exposure
    12.2 Time, distance, shielding concepts
    12.3 As low as reasonably achievable (ALARA) concept
    12.4 Radiation-detection equipment
    12.5 Exposure-device operating characteristics

Evaluation and Interpretation Course

1.0 Image Viewing
    1.1 Image display requirements
    1.2 Background lighting
    1.3 Multiple-composite viewing
    1.4 Image quality indicator (IQI) placement
    1.5 Personnel dark adaptation and visual acuity
    1.6 Image identification
    1.7 Location markers

2.0 Application Techniques
    2.1 Multiple-view techniques
        2.1.1 Thickness-variation parameters
    2.2 Enlargement and projection
    2.3 Geometric relationships
        2.3.1 Geometric unsharpness
        2.3.2 IQI sensitivity
        2.3.3 Source-to-detector distance
        2.3.4 Focal-spot size
    2.4 Triangulation methods for discontinuity location
    2.5 Localized magnification

3.0 Evaluation of Castings
    3.1 Casting-method review
    3.2 Casting discontinuities
    3.3 Origin and typical orientation of discontinuities

3.4   Casting codes/standards – applicable acceptance criteria

3.5   Reference radiographs or images

4.0   Evaluation of Weldments

    4.1   Welding-method review

    4.2   Welding discontinuities

    4.3   Origin and typical orientation of discontinuities

    4.4   Welding codes/standards – applicable acceptance criteria

    4.5   Reference radiographs or images

5.0   Standards, Codes and Procedures for Radiography

    5.1   ASTM standards

    5.2   Acceptable techniques and setups

    5.3   Applicable employer procedures

Radiological Testing Level III Topical Outline

Basic Radiology Topics

1.0   Principles/Theory

    1.1   Nature of penetrating radiation

    1.2   Interaction between penetrating radiation and matter

    1.3   Radiology overview

        1.3.1   Film radiography

        1.3.2   Computed radiography

        1.3.3   Computed tomography

        1.3.4   Digital radiography

            1.3.4.1   Radioscopy

2.0   Equipment/Materials

    2.1   Electrically generated sources

        2.1.1   X-ray sources

            2.1.1.1   Generators and tubes as an integrated system

            2.1.1.2   Sources of electrons

            2.1.1.3   Electron accelerating methods

            2.1.1.4   Target materials and characteristics

            2.1.1.5   Equipment design considerations

            2.1.1.6   Microfocus sources

    2.2   Isotope sources

        2.2.1   Exposure devices

        2.2.2   Source changers

        2.2.3   Remote-handling equipment

        2.2.4   Collimators

        2.2.5   Specific characteristics

            2.2.5.1   Half-lives

            2.2.5.2   Energy levels

            2.2.5.3   Half-value layers

            2.2.5.4   Tenth-value layers

    2.3   Radiation detection overview

        2.3.1   Direct imaging

            2.3.1.1   Film overview

            2.3.1.2   Radioscopy overview

            2.3.1.3   X-ray image intensifier system

        2.3.2   Digital data acquisition/detectors

            2.3.2.1   Film digitizers

            2.3.2.2   Computed radiography (CR)

2.3.2.3　Digital radiography (DR)
2.3.2.4　Computed tomography (CT)
2.4　Manipulators
2.4.1　Manual versus automated
2.4.2　Multiple axis
2.4.3　Weight capacity
2.4.4　Precision
2.5　Visual perception
2.5.1　Spatial frequency
2.5.2　Contrast
2.5.3　Displayed brightness
2.5.4　Signal-to-noise ratio (SNR)
2.5.5　Probability of detection (POD) (single versus multiple locations, scanning)
2.5.6　Receiver operator characteristic (ROC) curves

3.0　Safety and Health
3.1　Exposure hazards
3.1.1　Occupational dose limits
3.2　Methods of controlling radiation exposure
3.2.1　Time
3.2.2　Distance
3.2.2.1　Inverse square law
3.2.3　Shielding
3.2.3.1　Half-value layers
3.2.3.2　Tenth-value layers
3.3　Operational and emergency procedures
3.4　Dosimetry and film badges
3.5　Gamma leak testing
3.6　Transportation regulations

Radiographic Testing

1.0　Techniques/Calibration
1.1　Imaging considerations
1.1.1　Sensitivity
1.1.2　Contrast and definition
1.1.3　Geometric factors
1.1.4　Intensifying screens
1.1.5　Scattered radiation
1.1.6　Source factors
1.1.7　Detection media
1.1.8　Exposure curves
1.2　Film Processing
1.2.1　Darkroom procedures
1.2.2　Darkroom equipment and chemicals
1.2.3　Film processing
1.3　Viewing of radiographs
1.3.1　Illuminator requirements
1.3.2　Background lighting
1.3.3　Optical aids
1.4　Judging radiographic quality
1.4.1　Density
1.4.2　Contrast
1.4.3　Definition
1.4.4　Artifacts
1.4.5　Image quality indicators
1.4.6　Causes and correction of unsatisfactory radiographs

1.5   Exposure calculations
1.6   Radiographic techniques
        1.6.1   Blocking and filtering
        1.6.2   Multi-film techniques
        1.6.3   Enlargement and projection
        1.6.4   Stereoradiography
        1.6.5   Triangulation methods
        1.6.6   Autoradiography
        1.6.7   Flash radiography
        1.6.8   In-motion radiography
        1.6.9   Control of diffraction effects
        1.6.10 Pipe welding exposures
               1.6.10.1   Contact
               1.6.10.2   Elliptical
               1.6.10.3   Panoramic
        1.6.11 Gaging
        1.6.12 Real-time imaging
        1.6.13 Image analysis techniques
        1.6.14 Image-object relationship

2.0   Interpretation/Evaluation
    2.1   Material considerations
        2.1.1   Materials processing as it affects use of item and test results
        2.1.2   Discontinuities, their causes and effects
        2.1.3   Radiographic appearance of discontinuities
        2.1.4   Nonrelevent indications
        2.1.5   Film artifacts
        2.1.6   Code considerations

3.0   Procedures

Common Digital System Elements and Digital Image Properties

1.0   Digital Image Properties
    1.1   Bits/bytes
    1.2   Pixels/voxels
    1.3   Image file formats and compression (JPEG, TIFF, DICONDE)
        1.3.1   Advantages/disadvantages
        1.3.2   Lossy versus lossless
    1.4   Sampling theory (digitizing)
        1.4.1   Pixel size (aperture)
        1.4.2   Pixel pitch
        1.4.3   Bit depth
        1.4.4   Nyquist theory

2.0   Digital System Specific: Components
    2.1   Computer
        2.1.1   Operator interface
        2.1.2   System controller
        2.1.3   Image processor
    2.2   Monitor and viewing environment
        2.2.1   Type of monitors/displays
        2.2.2   Limited bit-depth display
        2.2.3   Monitor resolution
        2.2.4   Monitor brightness and contrast
        2.2.5   Monitor testing
        2.2.6   Monitor calibration
        2.2.7   Viewing area and ergonomics

Computed Radiography Testing

4.3   Maintenance of CR systems
4.4   Technical requirements for inspection

5.0   CR Technical Development
     5.1   Hardware development
        5.1.1   Hard/soft cassette usage
        5.1.2   Image plate wear and damage
        5.1.3   Image plate artifacts
     5.2   Software development
     5.3   CR image optimization
        5.3.1   Laser spot size optimization
        5.3.2   Use of lead screens

6.0   Use of Digital Reference Images
     6.1   ASTM standards review
     6.2   Digital reference images installation
        6.2.1   Include reference image resolutions/pixel size
     6.3   Use of reference images and contrast normalization

7.0   Review of DR Industry Standards (i.e., ASTM)

Computed Tomography Testing

1.0   Advanced Theoretical Background
     1.1   Radon transform
     1.2   Sampling the radon transform
     1.3   Convolution principles – point spread function
     1.4   Reconstruction processes
        1.4.1   Convolution/backprojections
        1.4.2   Fourier reconstructions
        1.4.3   Fan/cone beam

2.0   Advanced Image Processing and Algorithm Analysis
     2.1   System performance analysis
        2.1.1   Modulation transfer function
        2.1.2   Contrast detail dose curves
        2.1.3   Effective energy

3.0   CT System Performance Measurements and Monitoring
     3.1   CT system trade spaces
     3.2   CT system selection
     3.3   Key parameters
        3.3.1   Trade-offs
        3.3.2   Scan plan development

Digital Radiography Testing

1.0   DR System Capabilities
     1.1   DR system overview
     1.2   DR versus film procedural steps
     1.3   Cost and environmental issues
     1.4   Film versus DR images
     1.5   Linearity and latitude
     1.6   Contrast and resolution

2.0   Measuring Image Fidelity
    2.1   Contrast and resolution
    2.2   Modulation transfer function (MTF)
    2.3   Signal-to-noise ratio (SNR)

3.0   Image Fidelity Indicators (System Characterization)
    3.1   Image quality indicators (IQIs): hole and wire types
    3.2   Line pair gages
    3.3   Phantoms
    3.4   Reference quality indicators (RQIs)
    3.5   TV test patterns

4.0   Detector Selection
    4.1   ASTM E 2597 data interpretation
        4.1.1   Frame rate, resolution, ghosting/lag, bit depth
        4.1.2   Basic spatial resolution
        4.1.3   Bad pixel characterization
        4.1.4   Contrast sensitivity
        4.1.5   Efficiency
        4.1.6   Specific material thickness
        4.1.7   Modulation transfer function (MTF)
        4.1.8   Signal-to-noise ratio (SNR)
    4.2   Additional detector selection criteria/parameters
        4.2.1   Frame rate
        4.2.2   Blooming
        4.2.3   Ghosting/latent image/lag
        4.2.4   Scatter sensitivity
        4.2.5   Bit depth
        4.2.6   Fabrication anomalies (i.e., bad pixels, chip grades, etc.)
        4.2.7   Radiation exposure tolerance

5.0   DR Image Quality Topics
    5.1   Calibration optimization
    5.2   Setting bad pixel limits versus application
    5.3   Image unsharpness and geometric magnification
        5.3.1   Determining required geometric magnification
        5.3.2   Geometry and geometric unsharpness
        5.3.3   Focal spot size measurement method
        5.3.4   Total image unsharpness
    5.4   SNR compensation for spatial resolution
        5.4.1   Frame averaging
        5.4.2   Binning
        5.4.3   X-ray spectrum optimization
            5.4.3.1   Filtering
            5.4.3.2   Beam collimation
            5.4.3.3   Beam energy
    5.5   Radiation damage management

6.0   Qualification of DR Procedures
    6.1   Qualification plan
    6.2   System performance characterization
        6.2.1   Process controls
    6.3   Technique documentation
    6.4   Technique validation

7.0   Use of Digital Reference Images
    7.1   ASTM standards review
    7.2   Digital reference images installation
        7.2.1   Include reference image resolutions/pixel size
    7.3   Use of reference images and contrast normalization

Training References
Radiological Testing, Level I, II and III

Annual Book of ASTM Standards, Volume 03.03, *Nondestructive Testing*. Philadelphia, PA: American Society for Testing and Materials. Latest edition.*

ASNT Level II Study Guide: Radiographic Testing Method. Columbus, OH: The American Society for Nondestructive Testing, Inc. Latest edition.*

ASNT Level III Study Guide: Radiographic Testing Method, Columbus, OH: The American Society for Nondestructive Testing, Inc. Latest edition.*

Bossi, R.H., F.A. Iddings and G.C. Wheeler, tech. eds., P.O. Moore, ed., *Nondestructive Testing Handbook*, third edition: Volume 4, *Radiographic Testing*. Columbus, OH: The American Society for Nondestructive Testing, Inc. 2002.*

Materials and Processes for NDT Technology. Columbus, OH: American Society for Nondestructive Testing, Inc. 1981.*

McCain, D., *ASNT Study Guide: Industrial Radiography Radiation Safety*. Columbus, OH: American Society for Nondestructive Testing, Inc. 2009.

McGuire, S.A. and C.A. Peabody. *Working Safely in Radiography*. Columbus, OH: The American Society for Nondestructive Testing, Inc. 2004.*

Mix, P.E. *Introduction to Nondestructive Testing: A Training Guide,* second edition. New York: John Wiley & Sons. 2005.

Nondestructive Evaluation and Quality Control: ASM Handbook, Volume 17. Metals Park, OH: ASM International. 1989.*

Radiography in Modern Industry, www.kodak.com/eknec/documents/87/0900688a802b3c87/Radiography-in-Modern-Industry.pdf. Rochester, NY: Eastman Kodak Co. 1980.

Schneeman, J.G. *Industrial X-ray Interpretation*. Evanston, IL: Intex Publishing Co. 1985.*

Staton, J. *Radiographic Testing Classroom Training Book* (PTP Series). Columbus, OH: The American Society for Nondestructive Testing, Inc. 2005.*

Supplement to Recommended Practice No. SNT-TC-1A (Q&A Book): Radiographic Testing Method. Columbus, OH: The American Society for Nondestructive Testing, Inc. Latest edition.*

Taylor, J.L., ed., *Basic Metallurgy for Non-Destructive Testing*, revised edition. Essex, England: W.H. Houldershaw, Ltd. (British Institute of Nondestructive Testing). 1988.*

Thielsch, H. *Defects and Failures in Pressure Vessels and Piping*. New York: R.E. Krieger Publishing. 1977.*

Welding Inspection Handbook. Miami, FL: American Welding Society. Latest edition.

Note: Technical papers on much of the subject material can be found in the journal of ASNT, *Materials Evaluation*. For specific topics, see the index of *Materials Evaluation*, on the ASNT Web site (www.asnt.org).

* Available from the American Society for Nondestructive Testing, Inc., Columbus, OH.

Limited Certification for Radiographic Film Interpretation Topical Outlines

Note: It is expected that the trainee whose job function requires working with radiation sources receive 40 hours of radiation safety training instruction prior to performing work in radiography. The safety training does not count toward technique training requirements. Basic radiation safety training should follow current government regulations. A Radiation Safety Topical Outline is available in Appendix A and can be used as guidance.

Radiographic Technique Course

1.0 Introduction
    1.1 Process of radiography
    1.2 Types of electromagnetic radiation sources
    1.3 Electromagnetic spectrum
    1.4 Penetrating ability or "quality" of X-rays and gamma rays
    1.5 X-ray tube – change of mA or kVp effect on "quality" and intensity

2.0 Basic Principles of Radiography
    2.1 Geometric exposure principles
        2.1.1 "Shadow" formation and distortion
        2.1.2 Shadow enlargement calculation
        2.1.3 Shadow sharpness
        2.1.4 Geometric unsharpness
        2.1.5 Finding discontinuity depth
    2.2 Radiographic screens
        2.2.1 Lead intensifying screens
        2.2.2 Fluorescent intensifying screens
        2.2.3 Intensifying factors
        2.2.4 Importance of screen-to-film contact
        2.2.5 Importance of screen cleanliness and care
    2.3 Radiographic cassettes
    2.4 Composition of industrial radiographic film

3.0 Radiographs
    3.1 Formation of the latent image on film
    3.2 Inherent unsharpness
    3.3 Arithmetic of radiographic exposure
        3.3.1 Milliamperage – distance-time relationship
        3.3.2 Reciprocity law
        3.3.3 Photographic density
        3.3.4 Inverse square law considerations
    3.4 Characteristic (Hurter and Driffield) curve
    3.5 Film speed and class descriptions
    3.6 Selection of film for particular purpose

4.0 Radiographic Image Quality
    4.1 Radiographic sensitivity
    4.2 Radiographic contrast
    4.3 Film contrast
    4.4 Subject contrast
    4.5 Definition
    4.6 Film graininess and screen mottle effects
    4.7 Image quality indicators

5.0 Exposure Techniques – Radiography
    5.1 Single-wall radiography

5.2 Double-wall radiography
    5.2.1 Viewing two walls simultaneously
    5.2.2 Offset double-wall exposure single-wall viewing
    5.2.3 Elliptical techniques
5.3 Panoramic radiography
5.4 Use of multiple-film loading
5.5 Specimen configuration

Film Quality and Manufacturing Processes Course

1.0 Darkroom Facilities, Techniques and Processing
    1.1 Facilities and equipment
        1.1.1 Automatic film processor versus manual processing
    1.2 Protection of radiographic film in storage
    1.3 Processing of film – manual
        1.3.1 Developer and replenishment
        1.3.2 Stop bath
        1.3.3 Fixer and replenishment
        1.3.4 Washing
        1.3.5 Prevention of water spots
        1.3.6 Drying
    1.4 Automatic film processing
    1.5 Film filing and storage
        1.5.1 Retention-life measurements
        1.5.2 Long-term storage
        1.5.3 Filing and separation techniques
    1.6 Unsatisfactory radiographs – causes and cures
        1.6.1 High film density
        1.6.2 Insufficient film density
        1.6.3 High contrast
        1.6.4 Low contrast
        1.6.5 Poor definition
        1.6.6 Fog
        1.6.7 Light leaks
        1.6.8 Artifacts
    1.7 Film density
        1.7.1 Step-wedge comparison film
        1.7.2 Densitometers

2.0 Indications, Discontinuities and Defects
    2.1 Indications
    2.2 Discontinuities
        2.2.1 Inherent
        2.2.2 Processing
        2.2.3 Service
    2.3 Defects

3.0 Manufacturing Processes and Associated Discontinuities
    3.1 Casting processes and associated discontinuities
        3.1.1 Ingots, blooms and billets
        3.1.2 Sand casting
        3.1.3 Centrifugal casting
        3.1.4 Investment casing
    3.2 Wrought processes and associated discontinuities
        3.2.1 Forgings
        3.2.2 Rolled products
        3.2.3 Extruded products

3.3 Welding processes and associated discontinuities
    3.3.1 Submerged arc welding (SAW)
    3.3.2 Shielded metal arc welding (SMAW)
    3.3.3 Gas metal arc welding (GMAW)
    3.3.4 Flux corded arc welding (FLAW)
    3.3.5 Gas tungsten arc welding (GTAW)

Radiographic Evaluation and Interpretation Course

1.0 Radiographic Viewing
    1.1 Film-illuminator requirements
    1.2 Background lighting
    1.3 Multiple-composite viewing
    1.4 Image quality indicator placement
    1.5 Personnel dark adaptation and visual acuity
    1.6 Film identification
    1.7 Location markers
    1.8 Film-density measurement
    1.9 Film artifacts

2.0 Application Techniques
    2.1 Multiple-film techniques
        2.1.1 Thickness-variation parameters
        2.1.2 Film speed
        2.1.3 Film latitude
    2.2 Enlargement and projection
    2.3 Geometric relationships
        2.3.1 Geometric unsharpness
        2.3.2 Image quality indicator sensitivity
        2.3.3 Source-to-film distance
        2.3.4 Focal-spot size
    2.4 Triangulation methods for discontinuity location
    2.5 Localized magnification
    2.6 Film-handling techniques

3.0 Evaluation of Castings
    3.1 Casting-method review
    3.2 Casting discontinuities
    3.3 Origin and typical orientation of discontinuities
    3.4 Radiographic appearance
    3.5 Casting codes/standards – applicable acceptance criteria
    3.6 Reference radiographs

4.0 Evaluation of Weldments
    4.1 Welding-method review
    4.2 Welding discontinuities
    4.3 Origin and typical orientation of discontinuities
    4.4 Radiographic appearance
    4.5 Welding codes/standards – applicable acceptance criteria
    4.6 Reference radiographs or pictograms

5.0 Standards, Codes and Procedures for Radiography
    5.1 Acceptable radiographic techniques and setups
    5.2 Applicable employer procedures
    5.3 Procedure for radiograph parameter verification
    5.4 Radiographic reports

Thermal/Infrared Testing Level I Topical Outline

Basic Thermal/Infrared Physics Course

1.0 The Nature of Heat – What Is It and How Is It Measured/Expressed?
    1.1 Instrumentation
    1.2 Scales and conversions

2.0 Temperature – What Is It and How Is It Measured/Expressed?
    2.1 Instrumentation
    2.2 Scales and conversions

3.0 Heat Transfer Modes Familiarization
    3.1 Heat conduction fundamentals
        3.1.1 Fourier's law of heat conduction (concept)
        3.1.2 Conductivity/resistance basics
    3.2 Heat convection fundamentals
        3.2.1 Newton's law of cooling (concept)
        3.2.2 Film coefficient/film resistance basics
    3.3 Heat radiation fundamentals
        3.3.1 Stefan-Boltzmann Law (concept)
        3.3.2 Emissivity/absorptivity/reflectivity/transmissivity basics (Kirchhoff's law)

4.0 Radiosity Concepts Familiarization
    4.1 Reflectivity
    4.2 Transmissivity
    4.3 Absorptivity
    4.4 Emissivity
    4.5 Infrared radiometry and imaging
    4.6 Spatial resolution concepts
        4.6.1 Field of view (FOV)
        4.6.2 Instantaneous field of view (IFOV) – ref. ASTM E 1149
        4.6.3 Spatial resolution for temperature measurement – the split response function (SRF)
        4.6.4 Measurement instantaneous field of view (MIFOV)
    4.7 Error potential in radiant measurements (an overview)

Basic Thermal/Infrared Operating Course

1.0 Introduction
    1.1 Thermography defined
    1.2 How infrared imagers work
    1.3 Differences among imagers and alternative equipment
    1.4 Operation of infrared thermal imager
        1.4.1 Selecting the best perspective
        1.4.2 Image area and lens selection for required details
        1.4.3 Optimizing the image
        1.4.4 Basic temperature measurement
        1.4.5 Basic emissivity measurement
    1.5 Operation of support equipment for infrared surveys

2.0 Checking Equipment Calibration with Blackbody References

3.0 Infrared Image and Documentation Quality
    3.1 Elements of a good infrared image
        3.1.1 Clarity (focus)
        3.1.2 Dynamic range of the image

3.1.3   Recognizing and dealing with reflections
3.1.4   Recognizing and dealing with spurious convection
3.2   Recording
    3.2.1   Videotape
    3.2.2   Photographic images
    3.2.3   Video photo cameras
    3.2.4   Digital recording
    3.2.5   Videoprinters

4.0   Support Data Collection
  4.1   Environmental data
  4.2   Emissivity
    4.2.1   Measurement
    4.2.2   Estimation
    4.2.3   Surface modification
  4.3   Surface reference temperatures
  4.4   Identification and other

Basic Thermal/Infrared Applications Course

1.0   Detecting Thermal Anomalies Resulting from Differences in Thermal Resistance (Quasi-Steadystate Heat Flow)
  1.1   Large surface-to-ambient temperature difference
  1.2   Small surface-to-ambient temperature difference

2.0   Detecting Thermal Anomalies Resulting from Differences in Thermal Capacitance, Using System or Environmental Heat Cycles

3.0   Detecting Thermal Anomalies Resulting from Differences in Physical State

4.0   Detecting Thermal Anomalies Resulting from Fluid Flow Problems

5.0   Detecting Thermal Anomalies Resulting from Friction

6.0   Detecting Thermal Anomalies Resulting from Non-homogeneous Exothermic or Endothermic Conditions

7.0   Field Quantification of Point Temperatures
  7.1   Simple techniques for emissivity
  7.2   Typical (high emissivity) applications
  7.3   Special problem of low emissivity applications

Thermal/Infrared Testing Level II Topical Outline

Intermediate Thermal/Infrared Physics Course

1.0   Basic Calculations in the Three Modes of Heat Transfer
  1.1   Conduction – principles and elementary calculation
    1.1.1   Thermal resistance – principles and elementary calculations
    1.1.2   Heat capacitance – principles and elementary calculations
  1.2   Convection – principles and elementary calculations
  1.3   Radiation – principles and elementary calculations

2.0   The Infrared Spectrum

2.1 Planck's law/curves
    2.1.1 Typical detected bands
    2.1.2 Spectral emissivities of real surfaces
    2.1.3 Effects due to semi-transparent windows and/or gasses
    2.1.4 Filters

3.0 Radiosity Problems
  3.1 Blackbodies – theory and concepts
  3.2 Emissivity problems
    3.2.1 Black body emissivity
    3.2.2 The gray body and the non-gray body
    3.2.3 Broadband and narrow-band emitter targets
    3.2.4 Specular and diffuse emitters
    3.2.5 Lambertian and non-Lambertian emitters (the angular sensitivity of emissivity)
    3.2.6 Effects of emissivity errors
  3.3 Calculation of emissivity, reflectivity and transmissivity (practical use of Kirchoff's law)
  3.4 Reflectivity problem
    3.4.1 Quantifying effects of unavoidable reflections
    3.4.2 Theoretical corrections
  3.5 Transmissivity problem
    3.5.1 Quantified effects of partial transmittance
    3.5.2 Theoretical corrections

4.0 Resolution Tests and Calculations
  4.1 IFOV, FOV and MIFOV measurements and calculations
  4.2 MRTD measurements and calculations
  4.3 Slit response function – measurement, calculations, interpretations and comparisons
  4.4 Resolution versus lens and distance
  4.5 Dynamic range
  4.6 Data acquisition rate/data density
  4.7 Frame rate and field rate
  4.8 Image data density
    4.8.1 Lines of resolution
    4.8.2 IFOVs/line
    4.8.3 Computer pixels/line

Intermediate Thermal/Infrared Operating Course

1.0 Operating for Infrared Measurements (Quantification)
  1.1 Simple infrared energy measurement
  1.2 Quantifying the emissivity of the target surface
  1.3 Quantifying temperature profiles
    1.3.1 Use of black body temperature references in the image
    1.3.2 Use of temperature measurement devices for reference surface temperatures
    1.3.3 Common sources of temperature measurement errors
  1.4 Computer processing to enhance imager data

2.0 Operating for High-Speed Data Collection
  2.1 Producing accurate images of transient processes
  2.2 Recording accurate images of transient processes
  2.3 Equipment selection and operation for imaging from moving vehicles

3.0 Operating Special Equipment for "Active" Techniques
  3.1 Hot or cold fluid energy sources
  3.2 Heat lamp energy sources
  3.3 Flash-lamp energy sources
  3.4 Electromagnetic induction
  3.5 Laser energy sources

4.0 Reports and Documentation
   4.1 Calibration requirements and records
   4.2 Report data requirements
   4.3 Preparing reports

Intermediate Thermal/Infrared Applications Course

1.0 Temperature Measurement Applications
   1.1 Isotherms/alarm levels – personnel safety audits, etc.
   1.2 Profiles

2.0 Energy Loss Analysis Applications
   2.1 Conduction losses through envelopes
      2.1.1 Basic envelope heat-flow quantification
      2.1.2 Recognizing and dealing with wind effects
   2.2 Mass-transfer heat exchange (air or other flows into or out of the system)
      2.2.1 Location
      2.2.2 Quantification

3.0 "Active" Applications
   3.1 Insulation flaws
   3.2 Delamination of composites
   3.3 Bond quality of coatings
   3.4 Location of high heat-capacity components

4.0 Filtered Applications
   4.1 Sunlight
   4.2 Furnace interiors
   4.3 Semi-transparent targets

5.0 Transient Applications
   5.1 Imaging a rapidly moving process
   5.2 Imaging from a vehicle

Thermal/Infrared Testing Level III Topical Outline

1.0 Principles/Theory
   1.1 Conduction
   1.2 Convection
   1.3 Radiation
   1.4 The nature of heat and flow
      1.4.1 Exothermic or endothermic conditions
      1.4.2 Friction
      1.4.3 Variations in fluid flow
      1.4.4 Variations in thermal resistance
      1.4.5 Thermal capacitance
   1.5 Temperature measurement principles
   1.6 Proper selection of thermal/infrared testing (TIR) as technique of choice
      1.6.1 Differences between TIR and other techniques
      1.6.2 Complementary roles of TIR and other methods
      1.6.3 Potential for conflicting results between methods
      1.6.4 Factors that qualify/disqualify the use of TIR

2.0 Equipment/Materials
   2.1 Temperature measurement equipment
      2.1.1 Liquid – in-glass thermometers
      2.1.2 Vapor – pressure thermometers

3.4 Thermal/infrared imaging
    3.4.1 Calibration of equipment
    3.4.2 Quantifying emissivity
    3.4.3 Evaluating background radiation
    3.4.4 Measuring (or mapping) surface radiant energy
    3.4.5 Measuring (or mapping) surface temperatures
    3.4.6 Measuring (or mapping) surface heat flows
    3.4.7 Use in high temperature environments
    3.4.8 Use in high magnetic field environments
    3.4.9 Measurements on small targets
    3.4.10 Measurements through semitransparent materials

3.5 Heat flux indicators
    3.5.1 Calibration of equipment
    3.5.2 Measurement of heat flow

3.6 Exothermic or endothermic investigations. Typical examples may include, but are not limited to, the following:
    3.6.1 Power distribution systems
        3.6.1.1 Exposed electrical switchgear
        3.6.1.2 Enclosed electrical switchgear
        3.6.1.3 Exposed electrical busses
        3.6.1.4 Enclosed electrical busses
        3.6.1.5 Transformers
        3.6.1.6 Electric rotating equipment
        3.6.1.7 Overhead power lines
        3.6.1.8 Coils
        3.6.1.9 Capacitors
        3.6.1.10 Circuit breakers
        3.6.1.11 Indoor wiring
        3.6.1.12 Motor control center starters
        3.6.1.13 Lighter arrestors
    3.6.2 Chemical processes
    3.6.3 Foam-in-place insulation
    3.6.4 Fire fighting
        3.6.4.1 Building investigations
        3.6.4.2 Outside ground base investigations
        3.6.4.3 Outside airborne investigations
    3.6.5 Moisture in airframes
    3.6.6 Underground investigations
        3.6.6.1 Airborne coal mine fires
        3.6.6.2 Utility locating
        3.6.6.3 Utility pipe leak detection
        3.6.6.4 Void detection
    3.6.7 Locating and mapping utilities concealed in structures
    3.6.8 Mammal location and monitoring
        3.6.8.1 Ground investigations
        3.6.8.2 Airborne investigations
        3.6.8.3 Sorting mammals according to stress levels
    3.6.9 Fracture dynamics
    3.6.10 Process heating or cooling
        3.6.10.1 Rate
        3.6.10.2 Uniformity
    3.6.11 Heat tracing or channelized cooling
    3.6.12 Radiant heating
    3.6.13 Electronic components
        3.6.13.1 Assembled circuit boards
        3.6.13.2 Bare printed circuit boards
        3.6.13.3 Semiconductor microcircuits
    3.6.14 Welding

            3.6.14.1   Welding technique parameters

            3.6.14.2   Material parameters

      3.6.15   Mapping of energy fields

            3.6.15.1   Electromagnetic fields

            3.6.15.2   Electromagnetic heating processes

            3.6.15.3   Radiant heat flux distribution

            3.6.15.4   Acoustic fields

      3.6.16   Gaseous plumes

            3.6.16.1   Monitoring

            3.6.16.2   Mapping

      3.6.17   Ground frostline mapping

3.7   Friction investigations. Typical examples may include, but are not limited to, the following:

      3.7.1   Bearings

      3.7.2   Seals

      3.7.3   Drive belts

      3.7.4   Drive couplings

      3.7.5   Exposed gears

      3.7.6   Gearboxes

      3.7.7   Machining processes

      3.7.8   Aerodynamic heating

3.8   Fluid flow investigations. Typical examples may include, but are not limited to, the following:

      3.8.1   Fluid piping

      3.8.2   Valves

      3.8.3   Heat exchangers

      3.8.4   Fin fans

      3.8.5   Cooling ponds

      3.8.6   Cooling towers

      3.8.7   Distillation towers

            3.8.7.1   Packed

            3.8.7.2   Trays

      3.8.8   HVAC systems

      3.8.9   Lake and ocean current mapping

      3.8.10   Mapping civil and industrial outflows into waterways

      3.8.11   Locating leaks in pressure systems

      3.8.12   Filters

3.9   Thermal resistance (steady-state heat flow) investigations. Typical examples may include, but are not limited to, the following:

      3.9.1   Thermal safety audits

      3.9.2   Low temperature insulating systems

      3.9.3   Industrial insulation systems

      3.9.4   Refractory systems

      3.9.5   Semi-transparent walls

      3.9.6   Furnace interiors

      3.9.7   Disbonds in lined process equipment

3.10   Thermal capacitance investigations. Typical examples may include, but are not limited to, the following:

      3.10.1   Tank levels

      3.10.2   Rigid injection molding

      3.10.3   Thermal laminating processes

      3.10.4   Building envelopes

      3.10.5   Roof moisture

            3.10.5.1   Roof level investigations

            3.10.5.2   Airborne investigations

      3.10.6   Underground voids

      3.10.7   Bridge deck laminations

      3.10.8   Steam traps

      3.10.9   Paper manufacturing moisture profiles

      3.10.10 Subsurface discontinuity detection in materials

      3.10.11 Coating disbond

      3.10.12 Structural materials

        3.10.12.1 Subsurface discontinuity detection
        3.10.12.2 Thickness variations
        3.10.12.3 Disbonding

4.0   Interpretation/Evaluation
    4.1   Exothermic or endothermic investigation: Typical examples may include, but are not limited to, the examples shown in Section 3.6
    4.2   Friction investigations: Typical examples may include, but are not limited to, the examples shown in Section 3.7
    4.3   Fluid flow investigations: Typical examples may include, but are not limited to, the examples shown in Section 3.8
    4.4   Differences in thermal resistance (steady-state heat flow) investigations: Typical examples may include, but are not limited to, the examples shown in Section 3.9
    4.5   Thermal capacitance investigations: Typical examples may include, but are not limited to, the examples shown in Section 3.10

5.0   Procedures
    5.1   Existing codes and standards
    5.2   Elements of thermal/infrared testing job procedure development

6.0   Safety and Health
    6.1   Safety responsibility and authority
    6.2   Safety for personnel
        6.2.1   Liquefied nitrogen handling
        6.2.2   Compressed gas handling
        6.2.3   Battery handling
        6.2.4   Safety clothing
        6.2.5   Safety ropes and harnesses
        6.2.6   Ladders
        6.2.7   Safety backup personnel
    6.3   Safety for client and facilities
    6.4   Safety for testing equipment

Training References
Thermal/Infrared Testing, Level I, II and III

Primary Body of Knowledge References

Annual Book of ASTM Standards, Volume 03.03, *Nondestructive Testing*. Philadelphia, PA: American Society for Testing and Materials. Latest Edition.*

Annual Book of ASTM Standards, Volume 04.06, *Thermal Insulation; Environmental Acoustics*. Philadelphia, PA: American Society for Testing and Materials. Latest Edition.*

ASNT Level III Study Guide: Infrared and Thermal Testing. American Society for Nondestructive Testing, Inc. Latest edition.*

Maldague, X.P.V., tech. ed., and P.O. Moore, ed. *Nondestructive Testing Handbook,* third editon: Volume 3, *Infrared and Thermal Testing*. Columbus, OH: American Society for Nondestructive Testing, Inc. 2001.*

NFPA 70B *Recommended Practice for Electrical Equipment Maintenance*. National Fire Protection Association, Latest edition.

NFPA 70E *Standard for Electrical Safety on the Workplace*. National Fire Protection Association. Latest edition.

Secondary References

DeWitt, D.P. and G.D. Nutter, eds. *Theory and Practice of Radiation Thermometry*. New York: John Wiley & Sons, Inc. 1989.

Guyer, E.C. *Handbook of Applied Thermal Design*. Philadelphia: PA. Taylor & Francis. 1999.

Henderson, F.M. and A.J. Lewis, eds., R.A. Ryerson, ed. in chief. *Principles & Applications of Imaging Radar,* Volume 2. New York: John Wiley & Sons, Inc. 1998.

Holman, J.P. *Experimental Methods for Engineers*. New York: McGraw-Hill. 2000.

Holst, G.C. *Testing and Evaluation of Infrared Imaging Systems*, third edition. Winter Park, FL: SPIE Press and JCD Publishing Co. 1998.*

Holst, G.C. *Common Sense Approach to Thermal Imaging Systems*. Winter Park, FL: SPIE Press and JCD Publishing Co. 2001.*

Incropera, F.P. and D.P. DeWitt. *Fundamentals of Heat and Mass Transfer*, fifth edition. New York: John Wiley & Sons, Inc. 2001.*

Johnson, M., ed. *Earth Observing Platforms & Sensors,* Volume 1.1. New York: John Wiley & Sons, Inc. 2009.

Kaplan, Ht. *Practical Applications of Infrared Thermal Sensing and Imaging Equipment*, third edition. Tutorial Texts in Optical Engineering, Volume TT 75. Bellingham, WA: SPIE Press. 2007.

Maldague, X.P.V. *Theory and Practice of Infrared Technology for Nondestructive Evaluation*. New York: John Wiley & Sons. 2001.

Manual for Thermographic Analysis of Building Enclosures. 149-GP-2MP. Committee on Thermography. Canadian General Standards Board. 1986.

Schlessinger, M. and I.J. Spiro. *Infrared Technology Fundamentals, Optical Engineering Series/46*, second edition. CRC Press. 1994.

Thomas, R.A. *The Thermography Monitoring Handbook*, first edition. Coxmoor Publishing Company. 1999.

Tipler, P.A. and RA. Liewellyn. *Modern Physics*, fifth edition. W.H. Freeman. 2007.

Von Baeyer, H.C. *Warmth Disperses and Time Passes – The History of Heat*. Modern Library. 1999.

Wolfe, W.L. and G.J. Ziessis, eds. *The Infrared Handbook*. The Environmental Research Institute of Michigan (prepared for The Department of the Navy). 1985.

*   Available from the American Society for Nondestructive Testing, Inc., Columbus, OH.

Ultrasonic Level I Topical Outline

Basic Ultrasonic Course

Note: It is recommended that the trainee receive instruction in this course prior to performing work in ultrasonics.

1.0   Introduction
    1.1   Definition of ultrasonics
    1.2   History of ultrasonic testing
    1.3   Applications of ultrasonic energy
    1.4   Basic math review
    1.5   Responsibilities of levels of certification

2.0   Basic Principles of Acoustics
    2.1   Nature of sound waves
    2.2   Modes of sound-wave generation
    2.3   Velocity, frequency and wavelength of sound waves
    2.4   Attenuation of sound waves
    2.5   Acoustic impedance
    2.6   Reflection

2.7 Refraction and mode conversion
2.8 Snell's law and critical angles
2.9 Fresnel and fraunhofer effects

3.0 Equipment
   3.1 Basic pulse-echo instrumentation (A-scan, B-scan, C-scan and computerized systems)
      3.1.1 Electronics – time base, pulser, receiver and various monitor displays
      3.1.2 Control functions
      3.1.3 Calibration
         3.1.3.1 Basic instrument calibration
         3.1.3.2 Calibration blocks (types and use)
   3.2 Digital thickness instrumentation
   3.3 Transducer operation and theory
      3.3.1 Piezoelectric effect
      3.3.2 Types of transducer elements
      3.3.3 Frequency (transducer elements -thickness relationships)
      3.3.4 Near field and far field
      3.3.5 Beam spread
      3.3.6 Construction, materials and shapes
      3.3.7 Types (straight, angle, dual, etc.)
      3.3.8 Beam-intensity characteristics
      3.3.9 Sensitivity, resolution and damping
      3.3.10 Mechanical vibration into part
      3.3.11 Other type of transducers (Laser UT, EMAT, etc.)
   3.4 Couplants
      3.4.1 Purpose and principles
      3.4.2 Materials and their efficiency

4.0 Basic Testing Methods
   4.1 Contact
   4.2 Immersion
   4.3 Air coupling

Ultrasonic Technique Course

1.0 Testing Methods
   1.1 Contact
      1.1.1 Straight beam
      1.1.2 Angle beam
      1.1.3 Surface-wave and plate waves
      1.1.4 Pulse-echo transmission
      1.1.5 Multiple transducer
      1.1.6 Curved surfaces
         1.1.6.1 Flat entry surfaces
         1.1.6.2 Cylindrical and tubular shapes
   1.2 Immersion
      1.2.1 Transducer in water
      1.2.2 Water column, wheels, etc.
      1.2.3 Submerged test part
      1.2.4 Sound beam path – transducer to part
      1.2.5 Focused transducers
      1.2.6 Curved surfaces
      1.2.7 Plate waves
      1.2.8 Pulse-echo and through-transmission
   1.3 Comparison of contact and immersion methods

2.0 Calibration (Electronic and Functional)

2.1 Equipment
    2.1.1 Monitor displays (amplitude, sweep, etc.)
    2.1.2 Recorders
    2.1.3 Alarms
    2.1.4 Automatic and semiautomatic systems
    2.1.5 Electronic distance/amplitude correction
    2.1.6 Transducers

2.2 Calibration of equipment electronics
    2.2.1 Variable effects
    2.2.2 Transmission accuracy
    2.2.3 Calibration requirements
    2.2.4 Calibration reflectors

2.3 Inspection calibration
    2.3.1 Comparison with reference blocks
    2.3.2 Pulse-echo variables
    2.3.3 Reference for planned tests (straight beam, angle beam, etc.)
    2.3.4 Transmission factors
    2.3.5 Transducer
    2.3.6 Couplants
    2.3.7 Materials

3.0 Straight Beam Examination to Specific Procedures
    3.1 Selection of parameters
    3.2 Test standards
    3.3 Evaluation of results
    3.4 Test reports

4.0 Angle Beam Examination to Specific Procedures
    4.1 Selection of parameters
    4.2 Test standards
    4.3 Evaluation of results
    4.4 Test reports

Ultrasonic Testing Level II Topical Outline

Ultrasonic Evaluation Course

1.0 Review of Ultrasonic Technique Course
    1.1 Principles of ultrasonics
    1.2 Equipment
        1.2.1 A-scan
        1.2.2 B-scan
        1.2.3 C-scan
        1.2.4 Computerized systems
    1.3 Testing techniques
    1.4 Calibration
        1.4.1 Straight beam
        1.4.2 Angle beam
        1.4.3 Resonance
        1.4.4 Special applications

2.0 Evaluation of Base-Material Product Forms
    2.1 Ingots
        2.1.1 Process review
        2.1.2 Types, origin and typical orientation of discontinuities
        2.1.3 Response of discontinuities to ultrasound
        2.1.4 Applicable codes/standards

2.2 Plate and sheet
    2.2.1 Rolling process
    2.2.2 Types, origin and typical orientation of discontinuities
    2.2.3 Response of discontinuities to ultrasound
    2.2.4 Applicable codes/standards

2.3 Bar and rod
    2.3.1 Forming process
    2.3.2 Types, origin and typical orientation of discontinuities
    2.3.3 Response of discontinuities to ultrasound
    2.3.4 Applicable codes/standards

2.4 Pipe and tubular products
    2.4.1 Manufacturing process
    2.4.2 Types, origin and typical orientation of discontinuities
    2.4.3 Response of discontinuities to ultrasound
    2.4.4 Applicable codes/standards

2.5 Forgings
    2.5.1 Process review
    2.5.2 Types, origin and typical orientation of discontinuities
    2.5.3 Response of discontinuities to ultrasound
    2.5.4 Applicable codes/standards

2.6 Castings
    2.6.1 Process review
    2.6.2 Types, origin and typical orientation of discontinuities
    2.6.3 Response of ultrasound to discontinuities
    2.6.4 Applicable codes/standards

2.7 Composite structures
    2.7.1 Process review
    2.7.2 Types, origin and typical orientation of discontinuities
    2.7.3 Response of ultrasound to discontinuities
    2.7.4 Applicable codes/standards

2.8 Other product forms as applicable – rubber, glass, etc.

3.0 Evaluation of Weldments
    3.1 Welding processes
    3.2 Weld geometries
    3.3 Welding discontinuities
    3.4 Origin and typical orientation of discontinuities
    3.5 Response of discontinuities to ultrasound
    3.6 Applicable codes/standards

4.0 Evaluation of Bonded Structures
    4.1 Manufacturing processes
    4.2 Types of discontinuities
    4.3 Origin and typical orientation of discontinuities
    4.4 Response of discontinuities to ultrasound
    4.5 Applicable codes/standards

5.0 Discontinuity Detection
    5.1 Sensitivity to reflections
        5.1.1 Size, type and location of discontinuities
        5.1.2 Techniques used in detection
        5.1.3 Wave characteristics
        5.1.4 Material and velocity
    5.2 Resolution
        5.2.1 Standard reference comparisons
        5.2.2 History of part
        5.2.3 Probability of type of discontinuity
        5.2.4 Degrees of operator discrimination
        5.2.5 Effects of ultrasonic frequency
        5.2.6 Damping effects

5.3 Determination of discontinuity size
    5.3.1 Various monitor displays and meter indications
    5.3.2 Transducer movement versus display
    5.3.3 Two-dimensional testing techniques
    5.3.4 Signal patterns
5.4 Location of discontinuity
    5.4.1 Various monitor displays
    5.4.2 Amplitude and linear time
    5.4.3 Search technique

6.0 Evaluation
    6.1 Comparison procedures
        6.1.1 Standards and references
        6.1.2 Amplitude, area and distance relationship
        6.1.3 Application of results of other NDT methods
    6.2 Object appraisal
        6.2.1 History of part
        6.2.2 Intended use of part
        6.2.3 Existing and applicable code interpretation
        6.2.4 Type of discontinuity and location

Phased Array Level II Topical Outline

Note: It is recommended that this course have as a minimum prerequisite of an Ultrasonics Level II unrestricted certification.

The intent of this document is to provide "Basic" knowledge on phased array ultrasonic testing consistent with other methods and to acknowledge phased array as unique enough to warrant an additional body of knowledge and qualification requirements.

Phased Array (PA) Evaluation Course

1.0 Introduction
    1.1 Terminology of PA
    1.2 History of PA – medical ultrasound, etc.
    1.3 Responsibilities of levels of certification

2.0 Basic Principles of PA
    2.1 Review of ultrasonic wave theory: longitudinal and shear wave
    2.2 Introduction to PA concepts and theory

3.0 Equipment
    3.1 Computer-based systems
        3.1.1 Processors
        3.1.2 Control panel including input and output sockets
        3.1.3 Block diagram showing basic internal circuit modules
        3.1.4 Multi-element/multi-channel configurations
        3.1.5 Portable battery operated versus full computer-based systems
    3.2 Focal law generation
        3.2.1 Onboard focal law generator
        3.2.2 External focal law generator
    3.3 Probes
        3.3.1 Composite materials
        3.3.2 Pitch, gap and size
        3.3.3 Passive planes
        3.3.4 Active planes

      7.1.3   Weld inspections
           7.1.3.1   Fabrication/inservice
           7.1.3.2   Differences in material: carbon steel, stainless steel, high-temperature nickel-chromium alloy, etc.
           7.1.3.3   Review of welding discontinuities
           7.1.3.4   Responses from various discontinuities
  7.2   Data presentations
      7.2.1   Standard (A-scan, B-scan and C-scan)
      7.2.2   Other (D-scan, S-scan, etc.)
  7.3   Data evaluation
      7.3.1   Codes/standards/specifications
      7.3.2   Flaw characterization
      7.3.3   Flaw dimensioning
      7.3.4   Geometry
      7.3.5   Software tools
      7.3.6   Evaluation gates
  7.4   Reporting
      7.4.1   Imaging outputs
      7.4.2   Onboard reporting tools
      7.4.3   Plotting, ACAD, etc.

Time of Flight Diffraction Level II Topical Outline

Note: It is recommended that this course have as a minimum prerequisite of an Ultrasonics Level II unrestricted certification.

The intent of this document is to provide "Basic" knowledge on TOFD ultrasonic testing consistent with other methods and to acknowledge TOFD as unique enough to warrant an additional body of knowledge and qualification requirements.

Time of Flight Diffraction (TOFD) Evaluation Course

1.0   Introduction
  1.1   Terminology of TOFD
  1.2   History of TOFD (e.g., M.G. Silk)
  1.3   Responsibilities of levels of certification

2.0   Basic Principles of TOFD
  2.1   Review of ultrasonic wave theory, refracted longitudinal waves
  2.2   Introduction to TOFD concepts and theory
  2.3   Technique limitations

3.0   Equipment
  3.1   Computer-based systems
      3.1.1   Processors
      3.1.2   Control panel including input and output sockets
      3.1.3   Block diagram showing basic internal circuit modules
      3.1.4   Portable battery-operated versus full computer-based systems
  3.2   Beam profile tools
      3.2.1   Probe center separation (PCS) calculators for FLAT material/components
      3.2.2   Probe center separation (PCS) calculators for CURVE surfaces
      3.2.3   Beam spread effects and control
      3.2.4   Multiple zone coverage and limitations
  3.3   Probes
      3.3.1   Composite materials
      3.3.2   Damping characteristics
      3.3.3   Selection of frequency and diameter
  3.4   Wedges

        3.4.1   Incident and refracted angle selections
        3.4.2   High-temperature applications
    3.5   Scanners
        3.5.1   Mechanized
        3.5.2   Manual

4.0   Testing Techniques
    4.1   Line scans (single tandem probe setups)
    4.2   Line scans (multiple probe setups)
    4.3   Raster scans

5.0   Calibration
    5.1   Material velocity calculations
    5.2   Combined probe delay(s) calculation(s)
    5.3   Digitization rates and sampling
    5.4   Signal averaging
    5.5   Pulse width control
    5.6   PCS and angle selection
    5.7   Sensitivity
    5.8   Pre-amplifiers
    5.9   Effects of curvature

6.0   Data Collection
    6.1   Single probe setups
    6.2   Multiple probe setups
    6.3   Non-encoded scans
        6.3.1   Time-based data storage
    6.4   Encoded scans
        6.4.1   Line scans
        6.4.2   Raster scans
    6.5   Probe offsets and indexing

7.0   Procedures
    7.1   Specific applications
        7.1.1   Material evaluations
            7.1.1.1   Base material scans
        7.1.2   Weld inspections
            7.1.2.1   Detection and evaluation of fabrication welding flaws
            7.1.2.2   Detection and evaluation of inservice cracking
            7.1.2.3   Detection of volumetric loss such as weld root erosion and partial penetration weld dimensional verifications
            7.1.2.4   Geometric limitations
            7.1.2.5   Cladding thickness and integrity evaluations
        7.1.3   Complex geometries
            7.1.3.1   Transitions, nozzles, branch connections, tees, saddles, etc.
    7.2   Data presentations
        7.2.1   Standard (A-scan, D-scan)
        7.2.2   Other (B-scan, C-scan)
    7.3   Data evaluation
        7.3.1   Codes/standards/specifications
        7.3.2   Flaw characterization
        7.3.3   Flaw dimensioning
        7.3.4   Geometry
        7.3.5   Software tools
            7.3.5.1   Linearization
            7.3.5.2   Lateral/back wall straightening and removal
            7.3.5.3   Synthetic aperture focusing technique (SAFT)
            7.3.5.4   Spectrum processing
            7.3.5.5   Curved surface compensation
        7.3.6   Parabolic cursor(s)

7.4 Reporting
  7.4.1 Imaging outputs
  7.4.2 Onboard reporting tools
  7.4.3 Plotting, ACAD, etc.

Ultrasonic Testing Level III Topical Outline

1.0 Principles/Theory
  1.1 General
  1.2 Principles of acoustics
    1.2.1 Nature of sound waves
    1.2.2 Modes of sound wave generation
    1.2.3 Velocity, frequency and wavelength of sound waves
    1.2.4 Attenuation of sound waves
    1.2.5 Acoustic impedance
    1.2.6 Reflection
    1.2.7 Refraction and mode-conversion
    1.2.8 Snell's law and critical angles
    1.2.9 Fresnel and fraunhofer effects

2.0 Equipment/Materials
  2.1 Equipment
    2.1.1 Pulse-echo instrumentation
      2.1.1.1 Controls and circuits
      2.1.1.2 Pulse generation (spike, square wave and toneburst pulsers)
      2.1.1.3 Signal detection
      2.1.1.4 Display and recording methods, A-scan, B-scan and C-scan and digital
      2.1.1.5 Sensitivity and resolution
      2.1.1.6 Gates, alarms and attenuators
        2.1.1.6.1 Basic instrument calibration
        2.1.1.6.2 Calibration blocks
    2.1.2 Digital thickness instrumentation
    2.1.3 Transducer operation and theory
      2.1.3.1 Piezoelectric effect
      2.1.3.2 Types of transducer elements
      2.1.3.3 Frequency (transducer elements – thickness relationships)
      2.1.3.4 Near field and far field
      2.1.3.5 Beam spread
      2.1.3.6 Construction, materials and shapes
      2.1.3.7 Types (straight, angle, dual, etc.)
      2.1.3.8 Beam intensity characteristics
      2.1.3.9 Sensitivity, resolution and damping
      2.1.3.10 Mechanical vibration into parts
      2.1.3.11 Other types of transducers (Laser UT, EMAT, etc.)
    2.1.4 Transducer operation/manipulations
      2.1.4.1 Tanks, bridges, manipulators and squirters
      2.1.4.2 Wheels and special hand devices
      2.1.4.3 Transfer devices for materials
      2.1.4.4 Manual manipulation
    2.1.5 Resonance testing equipment
      2.1.5.1 Bond testing
      2.1.5.2 Thickness testing
  2.2 Materials
    2.2.1 Couplants
      2.2.1.1 Contact
        2.2.1.1.1 Purpose and principles
        2.2.1.1.2 Materials and their efficiency

4.0 Interpretations/Evaluations
- 4.1 Evaluation of base material product forms
    - 4.1.1 Ingots
        - 4.1.1.1 Process review
        - 4.1.1.2 Types, origin and typical orientation of discontinuities
        - 4.1.1.3 Response of discontinuities to ultrasound
        - 4.1.1.4 Applicable codes, standards, specs
    - 4.1.2 Plate and sheet
        - 4.1.2.1 Process review
        - 4.1.2.2 Types, original and typical orientation of discontinuities
        - 4.1.2.3 Response of discontinuities to ultrasound
        - 4.1.2.4 Applicable codes, standards, specs
    - 4.1.3 Bar and rod
        - 4.1.3.1 Process review
        - 4.1.3.2 Types, origin and typical orientation of discontinuities
        - 4.1.3.3 Response of discontinuities to ultrasound
        - 4.1.3.4 Applicable codes, standards, specs
    - 4.1.4 Pipe and tubular products
        - 4.1.4.1 Process review
        - 4.1.4.2 Types, origin and typical orientation of discontinuities
        - 4.1.4.3 Response of discontinuities to ultrasound
        - 4.1.4.4 Applicable codes, standards, specs
    - 4.1.5 Forgings
        - 4.1.5.1 Process review
        - 4.1.5.2 Types, origin and typical orientation of discontinuities
        - 4.1.5.3 Response of discontinuities to ultrasound
        - 4.1.5.4 Applicable codes, standards, specs
    - 4.1.6 Castings
        - 4.1.6.1 Process review
        - 4.1.6.2 Types, origin and typical orientation of discontinuities
        - 4.1.6.3 Response of discontinuities to ultrasound
        - 4.1.6.4 Applicable codes, standards, specs
    - 4.1.7 Composite structures
        - 4.1.7.1 Process review
        - 4.1.7.2 Types, origin and typical orientation of discontinuities
        - 4.1.7.3 Response of discontinuities to ultrasound
        - 4.1.7.4 Applicable codes standards, specs
    - 4.1.8 Miscellaneous product forms as applicable (rubber, glass, etc.)
        - 4.1.8.1 Process review
        - 4.1.8.2 Types, origin and typical orientation of discontinuities
        - 4.1.8.3 Response of discontinuities to ultrasound
        - 4.1.8.4 Applicable codes standards, specs
- 4.2 Evaluation of weldments
    - 4.2.1 Process review
    - 4.2.2 Weld geometries
    - 4.2.3 Types, origin and typical orientation of discontinuities
    - 4.2.4 Response of discontinuities to ultrasound
    - 4.2.5 Applicable codes, standards, specs
- 4.3 Evaluation of bonded structures
    - 4.3.1 Manufacturing process
    - 4.3.2 Types, origin and typical orientation of discontinuities
    - 4.3.3 Response of discontinuities to ultrasound
    - 4.3.4 Applicable codes/standards/specs
- 4.4 Variables affecting test results
    - 4.4.1 Instrument performance variations
    - 4.4.2 Transducer performance variations
    - 4.4.3 Test specimen variations
        - 4.4.3.1 Surface condition
        - 4.4.3.2 Part geometry
        - 4.4.3.3 Material structure

Training References
Ultrasonic Testing, Level I, II and III

ASNT Level III Study Guide: Ultrasonic Method. Columbus, OH: The American Society for Nondestructive Testing, Inc. Latest edition.*

Birks, A.S. and R.E. Green, Jr., tech. eds. P. McIntire, ed. *Nondestructive Testing Handbook*, second edition: Volume 7, *Ultrasonic Testing*. Columbus, OH: The American Society for Nondestructive Testing, Inc. 1991.*

Dube, N., ed. *Introduction to Phased Array Ultrasonic Technology Application*. R/T Tech. 2004.

Marks, P.T. *Ultrasonic Testing Classroom Training Book* (PTP Series). Columbus, OH: The American Society for Nondestructive Testing, Inc. 2007.*

ASNT Level II Study Guide: Ultrasonic Testing Method. Columbus, OH: The American Society for Nondestructive Testing, Inc. Latest edition.*

Supplement to Recommended Practice No. SNT-TC-1A (Q&A Book): Ultrasonic Testing Method. Columbus, OH: The American Society for Nondestructive Testing, Inc. Latest edition.*

Workman, G.L. and D. Kishoni, tech. eds., P.O. Moore, ed. *Nondestructive Testing Handbook*, third edition: Volume 7, *Ultrasonic Testing*. Columbus, OH: The American Society for Nondestructive Testing, Inc. 2007.*

*   Available from the American Society for Nondestructive Testing, Inc., Columbus, OH.

Limited Certification for Ultrasonic Digital Thickness Measurement Topical Outline

1.0 Principles/Theory
    1.1 General
    1.2 Principles of acoustics
        1.2.1 Nature of sound waves
        1.2.2 Modes of sound wave generation
        1.2.3 Velocity, frequency and wavelength of sound waves
        1.2.4 Attenuation/scattering of sound waves

2.0 Equipment/Materials
    2.1 Equipment
        2.1.1 Pulse-echo instrumentation
            2.1.1.1 Pulse generation
            2.1.1.2 Signal detection
            2.1.1.3 Display and recording methods, A-scan, B-scan, C-scan and digital
            2.1.1.4 Sensitivity and resolution
        2.1.2 Digital thickness instrumentation
        2.1.3 Transducer operation and theory
            2.1.3.1 Piezoelectric effect
            2.1.3.2 Frequency (crystal-thickness relationships)
            2.1.3.3 Types (straight, angle, single, dual, etc.)
    2.2 Materials
        2.2.1 Couplants
            2.2.1.1 Purpose and principles
            2.2.1.2 Material and their efficiency
        2.2.2 Calibration blocks
        2.2.3 Cables/connectors
        2.2.4 Test specimen

3.0 Techniques/Calibrations – Contact Straight Beam

4.0 Variables Affecting Test Results
    4.1 Instrument performance variations
    4.2 Transducer performance variations
    4.3 Test specimen variations
        4.3.1 Surface condition
        4.3.2 Part geometry
        4.3.3 Material structure

5.0 Procedure/Specification Applications/Thickness Measurement

Limited Certification for Ultrasonic A-scan Thickness Measurement Topical Outline

1.0 Principles/Theory
    1.1 General
    1.2 Principles of acoustics
        1.2.1 Nature of sound waves
        1.2.2 Modes of sound wave generation
        1.2.3 Velocity, frequency and wavelength of sound waves
        1.2.4 Attenuation of sound waves
        1.2.5 Acoustic impedance
        1.2.6 Reflection

2.0 Equipment/Materials
    2.1 Equipment
        2.1.1 Pulse-echo instrumentation
            2.1.1.1 Controls and circuits
            2.1.1.2 Pulse generation
            2.1.1.3 Signal detection
            2.1.1.4 Display and recording methods, A-scan, B-scan, C-scan and digital
            2.1.1.5 Sensitivity and resolution
            2.1.1.6 Gates, alarms and attenuators
            2.1.1.7 Basic instrument calibration
            2.1.1.8 Calibration blocks
        2.1.2 Digital thickness instrumentation
        2.1.3 Transducer operation and theory
            2.1.3.1 Piezoelectric effect
            2.1.3.2 Types of crystals
            2.1.3.3 Frequency (crystal-thickness relationships)
            2.1.3.4 Types (straight, angle, single, dual, etc.)
        2.1.4 Resonance testing equipment
            2.1.4.1 Thickness testing
    2.2 Materials
        2.2.1 Couplants
            2.2.1.1 Purpose and principles
            2.2.1.2 Material and their efficiency
        2.2.2 Calibration blocks
        2.2.3 Cables/connectors
        2.2.4 Test specimen
        2.2.5 Miscellaneous materials

3.0 Techniques/Calibrations – Contact Straight Beam
    3.1 Contact
        3.1.1 Straight beam
        3.1.2 Pulse-echo transmission

4.0 Variables Affecting Test Results
    4.1 Instrument performance variations
    4.2 Transducer performance variations
    4.3 Test specimen variations
        4.3.1 Surface condition
        4.3.2 Part geometry
        4.3.3 Material structure
    4.4 Personnel variations
        4.4.1 Skill level in interpretation of results
        4.4.2 Knowledge level in interpretation of results

5.0 Procedures
    5.1 Thickness measurement

Guided Wave Level I Topical Outline

Note: It is recommended that the trainee receive instruction in this course prior to performing work in guided wave testing

Guided wave (GW) or long-range ultrasonic testing is uniquely different and specialized such that it should be considered a separate technique for Level I and II personnel. The intent of this document is to provide basic body of knowledge requirements for guided wave testing consistent with other methods and not intended to replace specific training or schemes identified by the various equipment manufacturers.

Guided Wave Basic Theory

Guided Wave Level II Topical Outline

6.0 GW Data Analysis
    6.1   Advanced DAC and TCG
    6.2   Advanced spurious echoes
    6.3   Phase information
    6.4   Advanced C-scan display
    6.5   Testing under supports
    6.6   Temperature effect
    6.7   Reporting analysis results

7.0 Evaluation
    7.1   Comparison procedures
        7.1.1   Standards and references
        7.1.2   Application of results of other NDT methods
    7.2   Object appraisal
        7.2.1   History of pipe
        7.2.2   Intended use of pipe
        7.2.3   Existing and applicable code interpretation
        7.2.4   Type of discontinuity and location

Guided Wave Level III Topical Outline

1.0 Terminology of Guided Wave (GW)

2.0 Principles of GW
    2.1   Review of mathematical basics
        2.1.1   Advanced GW propagation theory
        2.1.2   Dispersion effect and compensation factors
        2.1.3   Effect of material properties
        2.1.4   Bi-layer systems
        2.1.5   Attenuation due to viscoelastic coatings and embedded medium (parameters affecting and mathematical prediction)
        2.1.6   Sensitivity to stiffness changes
        2.1.7   Properties of guided waves in cylindrical and toroidal structures
    2.2   Various types of GW modes
        2.2.1   Torsional, longitudinal and flexural
        2.2.2   Modes in bends

3.0 Equipment
    3.1   Advanced array configuration
    3.2   Transduction selection parameters
    3.3   Advanced calibration systems
    3.4   Underwater inspection
    3.5   GW monitoring
    3.6   Guided wave focusing
    3.7   Advanced transduction systems

4.0 Interpretations/Evaluations
    4.1   Identification of discontinuities in various industrial environments
    4.2   Variables affecting test results
        4.2.1   Transducer performance
        4.2.2   Instrument performance
        4.2.3   Effect of testing environment
        4.2.4   Pipe specifications (diameter, thickness, manufacturing method, tolerances) and condition (temperature, roughness, stress)
    4.3   Range and sensitivity
    4.4   Signal-to-noise ratio
    4.5   Detailed knowledge on how to classify and assess observations and identification of best NDT method for sizing (UT, RT, etc.) or monitoring defect growth (GW, UT, etc.)

5.0 Writing Procedures for Specific Applications
    5.1 General and bare or painted piping
    5.2 Insulated piping
    5.3 Inspection under supports (simple, welded, clamped)
    5.4 Road crossings
    5.5 Buried piping
    5.6 Plate
    5.7 Steel cable or wire rope
    5.8 Rods or rail stock
    5.9 Tubes

6.0 Understanding of Codes, Standards and Specifications

Training References
Guided Wave Testing, Level I, II and III

Achenbach, J.D. *Wave Propagation in Elastic Solids*. North Holland, New York. 1987.

Alleyne, D.N., B. Pavlakovic, M.J.S. Lowe and P. Cawley. "Rapid Long-Range Inspection of Chemical Plant Pipework Using Guided Waves," *Insight* Vol. 43. 2001. pp 93–96.

Puchot, A., C. Duffer, A. Cobb and G. Light, "Use of Magnetostrictive Sensor Technology for Testing Tank Bottom Floors," *Materials Evaluation*, June 2010, Vol. 68, No. 6.

Redwood, M. *Mechanical Wave-Guides, The Propagation of Acoustic and Ultrasonic Waves in Fluids and Solids with Boundaries*. New York: Pergamon. 1960.

Rose, J.L. *Ultrasonic Waves in Solid Media* Cambridge, UK: Cambridge University Press. 1999.

Rose, J.L. "Standing on the Shoulders of Giants: An Example of Guided Wave Inspection," *Materials Evaluation*. Vol. 60, No. 1. 2002. pp 53–59.

Vibration Analysis Testing Level I Topical Outline

Basic Vibration Analysis Physics Course

1.0 Introduction
    1.1 Brief history of NDT and vibration analysis
    1.2 The purpose of vibration analysis
    1.3 Basic principles of vibration analysis
    1.4 Basic terminology of vibration analysis to include:
        1.4.1 Measurement units
        1.4.2 Measurement orientation
        1.4.3 Hardware
        1.4.4 Software
        1.4.5 Machine components
        1.4.6 Data presentation

2.0 Transducers
    2.1 Types
    2.2 Applications
    2.3 Mounting
    2.4 Limitations

3.0 Instrumentation
   3.1   Types
   3.2   Applications
   3.3   Limitations

Basic Vibration Analysis Operating Course

1.0 Machinery Basics
   1.1   Machine types to include:
      1.1.1   Motors
      1.1.2   Pumps
      1.1.3   Gearbox
      1.1.4   Air handlers
      1.1.5   Compressors
      1.1.6   Turbines
      1.1.7   Rolls
   1.2   Machine components to include:
      1.2.1   Bearings
      1.2.2   Couplings
      1.2.3   Rotors
      1.2.4   Gears
      1.2.5   Impellers
      1.2.6   Belts/chains
   1.3   Machine orientations

2.0 Data Collection Procedures
   2.1   Upload/download route
   2.2   Following a route
   2.3   Data acquisition
      2.3.1   Recognize good versus bad data
      2.3.2   Perform machine observations
      2.3.3   Recognize abnormal conditions (exceptions data)

3.0 Safety and Health
   3.1   Mechanical
   3.2   Electrical
   3.3   Environmental
   3.4   Regulations
   3.5   Federal
   3.6   Local
   3.7   Equipments

Vibration Analysis Testing Level II Topical Outline

Intermediate Vibration Analysis Physics Course

1.0 Review
   1.1   Basic principles
   1.2   Basic terminology
   1.3   Transducers
   1.4   Instrumentation

2.0 Additional Terminology
   2.1   Data acquisition
   2.2   Signal processing
   2.3   Data presentation

3.0 Diagnostic Tools
   3.1 Phase
   3.2 Fast Fourier transform (FFT)
   3.3 Time waveform
   3.4 Orbit analysis
   3.5 Bode/nyquist
   3.6 Trend analysis

Intermediate Vibration Analysis Techniques Course

1.0 Data Acquisition
   1.1 Units
   1.2 Analysis parameters
   1.3 Alarm levels
   1.4 Time constant (minimum/maximum)
   1.5 Speed consideration
   1.6 Lines of resolution
   1.7 Overlap
   1.8 Number of averages (specifications)
   1.9 Averaging types and data collection methods
   1.10 Windows
   1.11 Sensitivity
   1.12 Special transducers
   1.13 Routes (data collection) and online systems
   1.14 Transducer selections
   1.15 Transducer location
   1.16 Types of data collection
   1.17 Resonance testing
   1.18 Check (instrument) calibration
   1.19 Codes, standards and specifications

2.0 Signal Processing
   2.1 Windows/weighting
      2.1.1 Hanning
      2.1.2 Uniform
   2.2 Overlap
   2.3 Filters
      2.3.1 High pass
      2.3.2 Low pass
      2.3.3 Bandpass
   2.4 Sampling rate and size
   2.5 Digital versus analog

3.0 Data Presentation
   3.1 Scope and limitations of different testing methods
   3.2 Waterfall/cascades
   3.3 Linear versus logarithmic
   3.4 Trends
   3.5 Changing units
   3.6 True zoom and expansion
   3.7 Order and/or frequency

4.0 Problem Identification
   4.1 Unbalance
   4.2 Misalignment
   4.3 Resonance
   4.4 Bearing defects
   4.5 Looseness

4.6 Bent shafts
4.7 Gear defects
4.8 Electrical defects
4.9 Hydraulic/flow dynamics
4.10 Rubs
4.11 Belts and couplings
4.12 Eccentricity

5.0 Reporting Methodology
5.1 Technical reports
5.2 Management-oriented reports
5.3 Oral reports

6.0 Safety and Health
6.1 Mechanical
6.2 Electrical
6.3 Environmental
6.4 Regulations
6.5 Federal
6.6 Local
6.7 Equipment

Vibration Analysis Testing Level III Topical Outline

The principles and theory section or any other section is not intended to be covered as a completely separate section. This category just means that somewhere in the material for training it is necessary to cover the basic theory and principles on those topics.

1.0 Principles/Theory
The vibration data provides detailed information about the condition of a machine and its components. Data can be processed and presented in different ways to help the analyst in diagnosing specific problems. The section on principles and theory provides the concepts of vibration analysis.
1.1 Physical concepts
1.1.1 Sources of vibration
1.1.2 Stiffness
1.1.3 Mass
1.1.4 Damping
1.1.5 Phase
1.1.6 Modes of vibration
1.1.7 Resonance
1.2 Data presentation
1.2.1 Units of measurement of spectrum
1.2.2 Waveform
1.2.3 Phase analysis
1.3 Sources of vibration
1.3.1 Reciprocating machinery analysis
1.3.2 Specialty machine concepts
1.3.2.1 Nonlinear behavior
1.4 Correction methods
1.4.1 Absorbers
1.4.2 Damping treatments

2.0 Equipment
This section under equipment includes instrumentation, sensors and cabling used in vibration analysis.
2.1 Sensors
2.1.1 Attachments (brackets, connectors, sensor mounting)
2.1.2 Cabling

2.2 Signal conditioning
2.3 Instruments
    2.3.1 Recorders
    2.3.2 Analyzers
    2.3.3 Oscilloscopes
    2.3.4 Multi-channel
2.4 Online monitoring
2.5 Equipment response to environments performance based
    2.5.1 Temperature gradients
    2.5.2 Moisture

3.0 Techniques/Calibration

Description of ways in which vibration analysis equipment can be used to perform vibration measurements and to analyze the results. This includes routine field calibration and correction of measured data due to effects of test equipment.

3.1 Calibration
    3.1.1 Point sensor calibration/verification
    3.1.2 Instrument calibration/verification
    3.1.3 Test instrument calibration/verification
3.2 Measurement and techniques
    3.2.1 Low speed
    3.2.2 High speed
    3.2.3 Variable
    3.2.4 Order tracking
    3.2.5 Time synchronous analysis
    3.2.6 Cross channel measurements
    3.2.7 Transient analysis
    3.2.8 Model analysis fundamentals (notice that)
    3.2.9 Operating deflection shape analysis
    3.2.10 Natural frequency tests
    3.2.11 Torsional vibration techniques
    3.2.12 Specialized vibration analysis techniques (demodulated spectrum, spike energy spectrum, etc.)
3.3 Correction techniques

Vibration correction techniques
    3.3.1 Add mass
    3.3.2 Alignment
    3.3.3 Clearances on journal bearings
    3.3.4 Correct beats
    3.3.5 Damping treatments
    3.3.6 Dynamic absorber
    3.3.7 Eliminate looseness
    3.3.8 Isolation treatments
    3.3.9 Speed change
    3.3.10 Stiffening

4.0 Analysis/Evaluation

Ability to analyze test data, perform an evaluation and recommend remedial action.

4.1 Data analysis
    4.1.1 Operational effects
    4.1.2 Correlation of test data
    4.1.3 Transient analysis
    4.1.4 In-depth time waveform analysis
    4.1.5 Cross channel analysis
    4.1.6 Multi-channel analysis
    4.1.7 Machinery specific analysis
4.2 Data evaluation
    4.2.1 Evaluation of data to standards/codes
    4.2.2 Specifications or acceptance criteria
    4.2.3 Failure mode and effects analysis

4.2.4   Root cause analysis

4.2.5   Cost justification or return on investment analysis

5.0   Procedures
To be able to develop procedures for performing the various types of testing techniques needed to determine equipment condition.

6.0   Safety and Health
Working in close proximity to operating equipment containing a great deal of energy, special care must be taken to avoid injury in addition to using specific personal protective equipment.
6.1   Mechanical
6.2   Electrical
6.3   Environmental
6.4   Regulations
6.5   Federal
6.6   Local
6.7   Equipment

Training References
Vibration Analysis Testing Method, Level I, II and III

API 610, 630, American Petroleum Institute.

Hydraulic Institute Application Standard, B-74-1.

Bloch, H. *Practical Machinery Management for Process Plants*, Volumes 1-4. Gulf Professional Publishing Co. 1998.

Crawford, A.R. *The Simplified Handbook of Vibration Analysis*, Volume I, *Introduction to Vibration Analysis*. Knoxville, TN: CSI. 1992.

Crawford, A.R. *The Simplified Handbook of Vibration Analysis*, Volume II, *Applied Vibration Analysis*. Knoxville, TN: CSI. 1992.

Eisenmann, R.C., Sr, and R.C. Eisenmann, Jr. *Machinery Malfunction Diagnosis and Correction: Vibration Analysis and Troubleshooting for Process Industries*. Upper Saddle River, NJ: Prentice Hall Printers. 1998.

Goldman, S. *Vibration Spectrum Analysis: A Practical Approach*. New York: Industrial Press. 1999.

Den Hartog, J.P. *Mechanical Vibrations*. Mineola, NY: Castre Press. 2008.

Harris, C.M. *Shock & Vibration Handbook*. McGraw-Hill Inc. 1995.

Jackson, C. *Practical Vibration Primer*. Gulf Publishing Co. 1979.

Mitchell, J.S. *An Introduction to Machinery Analysis and Monitoring*. Tulsa, OK: PenWell Publishing Co. 1993.

Schneider, H. *Balancing Technology*. Deer Park, NY: Schenck Trebel Corporation. 1991.

Taylor, J.I. *The Vibration Analysis Handbook*. Tampa, FL: Vibration Consultants. 2003.

Taylor, J.I. *The Bearing Analysis Handbook*. Tampa, FL: Vibration Consultants. 2003.

Taylor, J.I. *The Gear Analysis Handbook*. Tampa, FL: Vibration Consultants. 2003.

Wowk, V. *Machinery Vibration: Measurement and Analysis*. McGraw-Hill. 1991.

Wowk, V. *Machinery Vibration: Balancing*. McGraw-Hill. 1994.

Visual Testing Level I Topical Outline

Note: The guidelines listed below should be implemented using equipment and procedures relevant to the employer's industry. No times are given for a specific subject; this should be specified in the employer's written practice. Based upon the employer's product, not all of the referenced subcategories need apply.

1.0 Introduction
    1.1 Definition of visual testing
    1.2 History of visual testing
    1.3 Overview of visual testing applications

2.0 Definitions
    Standard terms and their meanings in the employer's industry

3.0 Fundamentals
    3.1 Vision
    3.2 Lighting
    3.3 Material attributes
    3.4 Environmental factors
    3.5 Visual perception
    3.6 Direct and indirect methods

4.0 Equipment (as applicable)
    4.1 Mirrors
    4.2 Magnifiers
    4.3 Borescopes
    4.4 Fiberscopes
    4.5 Videoprobes
    4.6 Remote visual inspection systems
    4.7 Light sources and special lighting
    4.8 Gages (welding, go/no-go, etc.) templates, scales, micrometers, calipers, special tools, etc.
    4.9 Automated systems
    4.10 Computer-enhanced systems

5.0 Employer-Defined Applications
    (Includes a description of inherent, processing and service discontinuities.)
    5.1 Mineral-based material
    5.2 Metallic materials, including welds
    5.3 Organic-based materials
    5.4 Other materials (employer defined)

6.0 Visual Testing to Specific Procedures
    6.1 Selection of parameters
        6.1.1 Inspection objectives
        6.1.2 Inspection checkpoints
        6.1.3 Sampling plans
        6.1.4 Inspection patterns
        6.1.5 Documented procedures
    6.2 Test standards/calibration
    6.3 Classification of indications per acceptance criteria
    6.4 Reports and documentation

Visual Testing Level II Topical Outline

The guidelines listed below should be implemented using equipment and procedures relevant to the employer's industry. The employer should tailor the program to the company's particular application area. Discontinuity cause, appearance, and how to best visually detect and identify these discontinuities should be emphasized. No times are given for a specific subject; this should be specified in the employer's written practice. Depending upon the employer's product, not all the referenced subcategories need apply.

1.0 Introduction of Visual Testing and Remote Visual Inspection
    1.1 History
    1.2 Applications
    1.3 Advantages and limitations

2.0 Fundamentals
    2.1 Vision
        2.1.1 Anatomy of the eye and mechanics of vision
    2.2 Vision limitations
        2.2.1 Perceptions
        2.2.2 Orientation
        2.2.3 Disorders
    2.3 Employer's visual acuity examination methods

3.0 Lighting
    3.1 Fundamentals of light
    3.2 Lighting measurements

4.0 Material Attributes
    4.1 Cleanliness
    4.2 Color
    4.3 Condition
    4.4 Shape
    4.5 Size
    4.6 Temperature
    4.7 Texture
    4.8 Type

5.0 Environmental and Physiological Factors
    5.1 Atmosphere
    5.2 Cleanliness
    5.3 Comfort
    5.4 Distance
    5.5 Elevation
    5.6 Fatigue
    5.7 Health
    5.8 Humidity
    5.9 Mental attitude
    5.10 Relative position
    5.11 Temperature
    5.12 Perception

6.0 Principles and Theory
    6.1 Optics
        6.1.1 Lens optics
        6.1.2 Fiber optics
    6.2 Video technology
        6.2.1 Video camera charged coupled devices (CCD)

7.0 Equipment
    7.1 Lighting
        7.1.1 Standard lighting
        7.1.2 Special lighting
    7.2 Direct
        7.2.1 Magnification
        7.2.2 Mirrors
        7.2.3 Gages, micrometers, calipers, templates, scales, etc.

7.3   *Indirect (remote)
    7.3.1   *Borescopes (lens optics)
    7.3.2   *Fiberscopes (fiber optics)
    7.3.3   *Combined scopes (lens and fiber systems)
    7.3.4   *Videoscopes (lens/fiber optics with integral CCD imager)
        7.3.4.1   *Videoscope measurement techniques
            7.3.4.1.1 *Comparison
            7.3.4.1.2 *Shadow
            7.3.4.1.3 *Stereo
        7.3.4.2   *Push-tube camera
        7.3.4.3   *Pipe-crawler camera system
        7.3.4.4   *Pan, tilt and zoom camera
    7.3.5   *Auxilary video equipment
        7.3.5.1   *Monitors
        7.3.5.2   *Processors
        7.3.5.3   *Cables

8.0   Applications and Techniques
    8.1   Recommended lighting levels
    8.2   Light techniques for inspection
    8.3   Metallic materials
        8.3.1   Welds
        8.3.2   Castings
        8.3.3   Forgings
        8.3.4   Extrusions
        8.3.5   Wrought/formed
        8.3.6   Mechanical connections
        8.3.7   Electrical connections
        8.3.8   Thermal connections
    8.4   Mineral-based material
        8.4.1   Ceramics
        8.4.2   Tiles
    8.5   Other materials and products
        8.5.1   Composites

9.0   Evaluation and Disposition Criteria
    9.1   Environmental
    9.2   Infrastructure
    9.3   Power generation
    9.4   Petrochemical processing
    9.5   Manufacturing
    9.6   Aviation
    9.7   Military

10.0   Visual Testing and Remote Visual Inspection Requirements
    10.1   Codes
    10.2   Standards
    10.3   Procedures

11.0   Recording and Documentation
    11.1   Technique reports
    11.2   Data reports
    11.3   Image recording methods
        11.3.1   Drawings and sketches on hard-copy mediums
        11.3.2   Photographic mediums
        11.3.3   Electronic image mediums
            11.3.3.1   Magnetic mediums (VHS, S-VHS, Mini Digital Cassette)
            11.3.3.2   Optical mediums (DVD)
            11.3.3.3   Digital mediums (compact flash, USB flash drive, smart media, secure digital, memory stick, etc.)

12.0 Terminology and Definitions

*   Topics may be deleted if the visual testing is only required to perform direct visual inspection.

Visual Testing Level III Topical Outline

1.0   Principles/Theory
    1.1   Vision and light
       1.1.1   Physiology of sight
       1.1.2   Visual acuity
       1.1.3   Visual angle and distance
       1.1.4   Color vision
       1.1.5   Physics and measurement of light
    1.2   Environmental factors
       1.2.1   Lighting
       1.2.2   Cleanliness
       1.2.3   Distance
       1.2.4   Air contamination
    1.3   Test object characteristics
       1.3.1   Texture
       1.3.2   Color
       1.3.3   Cleanliness
       1.3.4   Geometry

2.0   Equipment Accessories
    2.1   Magnifiers
    2.2   Mirrors
    2.3   Dimensional
       2.3.1   Linear measurement
       2.3.2   Micrometers/calipers
       2.3.3   Optical comparators
       2.3.4   Dial indicators
       2.3.5   Gages
    2.4   Borescopes
       2.4.1   Rigid
       2.4.2   Fiber optic
       2.4.3   Special purpose
    2.5   Video systems (robotics)
       2.5.1   Photoelectric devices
       2.5.2   Microscopy
       2.5.3   Video borescopes
       2.5.4   Video imaging/resolution/image processing (enhancement)
       2.5.5   Charge coupled devices (CCDs)
    2.6   Automated systems
       2.6.1   Lighting techniques
       2.6.2   Optical filtering
       2.6.3   Image sensors
       2.6.4   Signal processing
    2.7   Video technologies
    2.8   Machine vision
    2.9   Replication
    2.10   Surface comparators
    2.11   Chemical aids
    2.12   Photography
    2.13   Eye

3.0   Techniques/Calibration
    3.1   Diagrams and drawings
    3.2   Raw materials

Training References
Visual Testing, Level I, II and III

Allgaier, M.W. and S. Ness, tech. eds., P. MclIntire and P.O.k Moore, eds. *Nondestructive Testing Handbook*, second edition: Volume 8, *Visual and Optical Testing*. Columbus, OH: The American Society for Nondestructive Testing, Inc. 1993.*

Allgaier, M.W. and R.E. Cameron, tech. eds., P.O. Moore, ed. *Nondestructive Testing Handbook*, third edition: Volume 9, *Visual Testing*. Columbus, OH: The American Society for Nondestructive Testing, Inc. 2010.*

ASNT Level II Study Guide: Visual and Optical Testing Method. Columbus, OH: American Society for Nondestructive Testing, Inc, Latest edition.*

ASNT Level III Study Guide: Visual and Optical Testing Method. Columbus, OH: American Society for Nondestructive Testing, Inc. Latest edition.*

Cary, H.B. and S. Helzer. *Modern Welding Technology*. Englewood Cliffs, NJ: Prentice-Hall, Inc. 2004.

Nondestructive Evaluation and Quality Control: ASM Handbook, Volume 17. Metals Park, OH: ASM International. 1989.*

The Tools and Rules of Precision Measuring. Athol, MA: L.S. Starret Co. 1982.

Welding Handbook, Volume 1. Miami, FL: American Welding Society. Latest edition.

Welding Inspection. Miami, FL: American Welding Society. Latest edition.

*   Available from The American Society for Nondestructive Testing, Inc., Columbus, OH.

Basic Examination Level III Topical Outline

General Level III Requirements

The Basic examination will cover three main topical areas:
- 1.0   Personnel qualification and certification programs
  - 1.1   *Recommended Practice No. SNT-TC-1A*
  - 1.2   *ANSI/ASNT CP-189*
  - 1.3   ASNT Level III program
- 2.0   General familiarity with other NDT methods.
- 3.0   General knowledge of materials, fabrication and product technology.

Separate Method examinations will be given to cover each of the following NDT Methods:

Acoustic Emission Testing	Neutron Radiographic Testing
Electromagnetic Testing	Radiographic Testing
Leak Testing	Thermal/Infrared Testing
Liquid Penetrant Testing	Ultrasonic Testing
Magnetic Particle Testing	Visual Testing

Each of the ten Method examinations are divided into three main topical areas:
- 1.0   Method fundamentals and principles
- 2.0   General knowledge of techniques within the methods
- 3.0   General interpretation of codes, standards and specifications relating to the method

The Basic examination and one or more Method examinations must be taken and passed to qualify for an ASNT Level III Certificate. The endorsements on the ASNT Certificate will list the various Methods, which the applicant passed.

The following topical outlines further subdivide the main topical areas of both Basic and Method examinations, cite literature references, and have sample questions typical of those in the examinations.

Recommended Practice No. SNT-TC-1A
- 1.0   Scope
- 2.0   Definitions
- 3.0   Nondestructive testing methods
- 4.0   Levels of qualification
- 5.0   Written practice
- 6.0   Education, training and experience
- 7.0   Training programs
- 8.0   Examinations
- 9.0   Certification
- 10.0   Termination

ASNT Standard *ANSI/ASNT CP-189*
- 1.0   Scope
- 2.0   Definitions
- 3.0   Levels of qualification
- 4.0   Qualification requirements
- 5.0   Qualification and certification
- 6.0   Examinations
- 7.0   Expiration, suspension, revocation and reinstatement of employee's certification
- 8.0   Employer recertification
- 9.0   Records
- 10.0   Referenced publications

ASNT Level III Certification Program
- 1.0   Scope
- 2.0   Definitions
- 3.0   Certification outcome

Training References
Basic Level III

ASNT Level III Program Document (online on the ASNT/Certification Web page).**

ASNT Standard for Qualification and Certification of Nondestructive Testing Personnel, ANSI/ASNT CP-189. Columbus, OH: The American Society for Nondestructive Testing, Inc. Latest edition.*

ASNT Level III Study Guide: Basic. Columbus, OH: The American Society for Nondestructive Testing, Inc. Latest edition.*

Harris, D.W. *A Guide to Personnel Qualification and Certification*. Columbus, OH: The American Society for Nondestructive Testing, Inc. 2008.*

Recommended Practice No. SNT-TC-1A: Personnel Qualification and Certification in Nondestructive Testing. Columbus, OH: The American Society for Nondestructive Testing, Inc. Latest edition.*

*   Available from The American Society for Nondestructive Testing, Inc., Columbus, OH.
** Available online at www.asnt.org.

Basics of Common NDT Methods

1.0   Acoustic Emission Testing
    1.1   Fundamentals
        1.1.1   Principles/theory of acoustic emission testing
        1.1.2   Sources of acoustic emissions
        1.1.3   Equipment and material
    1.2   Proper selection of acoustic emission technique
        1.2.1   Instrumentation and signal processing
            1.2.1.1   Cables (types)
            1.2.1.2   Signal conditioning
            1.2.1.3   Signal detection
            1.2.1.4   Noise discrimination
            1.2.1.5   Electronic technique
            1.2.1.6   Attenuation materials
            1.2.1.7   Data filtering techniques
    1.3   Interpretation and evaluation of test results

2.0   Electromagnetic Testing
    2.1   Fundamentals
        2.1.1   Electromagnetic field generation
        2.1.2   Properties of eddy current
        2.1.3   Effects of varying frequency
        2.1.4   Phase discrimination
    2.2   Electromagnetic testing
        2.2.1   Sensors
        2.2.2   Basic types of equipment; types of read out
        2.2.3   Reference standards
        2.2.4   Applications and test result interpretation

6.1   Fundamentals
      6.1.1   Magnetic field principles
      6.1.2   Magnetization by means of electric current
      6.1.3   Demagnetization
6.2   Magnetic particle inspection
      6.2.1   Basic types of equipment and inspection materials
      6.2.2   Test results interpretation; discontinuity indications
      6.2.3   Applications
            6.2.3.1   Welds
            6.2.3.2   Castings
            6.2.3.3   Wrought metals
            6.2.3.4   Machined parts
            6.2.3.5   Field applications

7.0   Neutron Radiographic Testing
     7.1   Fundamentals
         7.1.1   Sources
             7.1.1.1   X-ray
             7.1.1.2   Isotopic
             7.1.1.3   Neutron
         7.1.2   Detectors
             7.1.2.1   Imaging
             7.1.2.2   Nonimaging
         7.1.3   Nature of penetrating radiation and interactions with matter
         7.1.4   Essentials of safety
     7.2   Neutron radiographic testing
         7.2.1   Basic imaging considerations
         7.2.2   Test result interpretation; discontinuity indications
         7.2.3   Systems factors (source/test object/detector interactions)
         7.2.4   Applications
             7.2.4.1   Explosives and pyrotechnic devices
             7.2.4.2   Assembled components
             7.2.4.3   Bonded components
             7.2.4.4   Corrosion detection
             7.2.4.5   Nonmetallic materials

8.0   Radiographic Testing
     8.1   Fundamentals
         8.1.1   Sources
             8.1.1.1   Castings
             8.1.1.2   Welds
             8.1.1.3   Assemblies
             8.1.1.4   Electronic components
             8.1.1.5   Field inspections
         8.1.2   Detectors
             8.1.2.1   Imaging
             8.1.2.2   Nonimaging
         8.1.3   Nature of penetrating radiation and interactions with matter
         8.1.4   Essentials of safety
     8.2   Radiographic testing
         8.2.1   Basic imaging considerations
         8.2.2   Test result interpretation; discontinuity indications
         8.2.3   Systems factors (source/test object/detector interactions)
         8.2.4   Applications
             8.2.4.1   Castings
             8.2.4.2   Welds
             8.2.4.3   Assemblies
             8.2.4.4   Electronic components
             8.2.4.5   Field inspections

9.0 Thermal/Infrared Testing
    9.1 Fundamentals
        9.1.1 Principles and theory of thermal/infrared testing
        9.1.2 Temperature measurement principles
        9.1.3 Proper selection of thermal/infrared technique
    9.2 Equipment/materials
        9.2.1 Temperature measurement equipment
        9.2.2 Heat flux indicators
        9.2.3 Non-contact devices
    9.3 Applications
        9.3.1 Contact temperature indicators
        9.3.2 Non-contact pyrometers
        9.3.3 Line-scanners
        9.3.4 Thermal imaging
        9.3.5 Heat flux indicators
        9.3.6 Exothermic or endothermic investigations
        9.3.7 Friction investigations
        9.3.8 Fluid flow investigations
        9.3.9 Thermal resistance investigations
        9.3.10 Thermal capacitance investigations
    9.4 Interpretation and evaluation

10.0 Ultrasonic Testing
    10.1 Fundamentals
        10.1.1 Ultrasonic sound beams
            10.1.1.1 Wave travel modes
            10.1.1.2 Refraction, reflection, scattering and attenuation
        10.1.2 Transducers and sound beam coupling
    10.2 Ultrasonic testing
        10.2.1 Basic types of equipment
        10.2.2 Reference standards
        10.2.3 Test result interpretation; discontinuity indications
        10.2.4 System factors
        10.2.5 Applications
            10.2.5.1 Flaw detection
            10.2.5.2 Thickness measurement
            10.2.5.3 Bond evaluation
            10.2.5.4 Process control
            10.2.5.5 Field inspection

11.0 Visual Testing
    11.1 Fundamentals
        11.1.1 Principles and theory of visual testing
        11.1.2 Selection of correct visual technique
        11.1.3 Equipment and materials
    11.2 Specific applications
        11.2.1 Metal joining processes
        11.2.2 Pressure vessels
        11.2.3 Pumps
        11.2.4 Valves
        11.2.5 Bolting
        11.2.6 Castings
        11.2.7 Forgings
        11.2.8 Extrusions
        11.2.9 Microcircuits
    11.3 Interpretation and evaluation
        11.3.1 Codes and standards
        11.3.2 Environmental factors

Training References
Basics of Common NDT Methods

Badger, D. *Liquid Penetrant Testing Classroom Training Book* (PTP Series). Columbus, OH: The American Society for Nondestructive Testing, Inc. 2005.*

Marks, P.T. *Ultrasonic Testing, Classroom Training Book* (PTP Series). Columbus, OH: The American Society for Nondestructive Testing, Inc. 2007

Mix, P.E. *Introduction to Nondestructive Testing: A Training Guide*, second edition. New York: John Wiley & Sons, Inc. 2005.

Ness, S. and C.N. Sherlock, tech. eds., P.O. Moore and P. McIntire, eds. *Nondestructive Testing Handbook*, second edition: Volume 10, *Nondestructive Testing Overview*. Columbus, OH: The American Society for Nondestructive Testing, Inc. 1996.*

Sadek, H. *Electromagnetic Testing Classroom Training Book* (PTP Series). Columbus, OH: The American Society for Nondestructive Testing, Inc. 2005.*

Smith, G. *Magnetic Particle Testing Classroom Training Book* (PTP Series). Columbus, OH: The American Society for Nondestructive Testing, Inc. 2004.*

Staton, J. *Radiographic Testing Classroom Training Book* (PTP Series). Columbus, OH: The American Society for Nondestructive Testing, Inc. 2005.*

* Available from The American Society for Nondestructive Testing, Inc., Columbus, OH.

Basic Materials, Fabrication and Product Technology

1.0 Fundamentals of Material Technology
    1.1 Properties of materials
        1.1.1 Strength and elastic properties
        1.1.2 Physical properties
        1.1.3 Material properties testing
    1.2 Origin of discontinuities and failure modes
        1.2.1 Inherent discontinuities
        1.2.2 Process-induced discontinuities
        1.2.3 Service-induced discontinuities
        1.2.4 Failures in metallic materials
        1.2.5 Failures in nonmetallic materials
    1.3 Statistical nature of detecting and characterizing discontinuities

2.0 Fundamentals of Fabrication and Product Technology
    2.1 Raw materials processing
    2.2 Metals processing
        2.2.1 Primary metals
            2.2.1.1 Metal ingot production
            2.2.1.2 Wrought primary metals
        2.2.2 Castings
            2.2.2.1 Green sand molded
            2.2.2.2 Metal molded
            2.2.2.3 Investment molded
        2.2.3 Welding
            2.2.3.1 Common processes
            2.2.3.2 Hard-surfacing
            2.2.3.3 Solid-state

2.2.4   Brazing
2.2.5   Soldering
2.2.6   Machining and material removal
    2.2.6.1   Turning, boring and drilling
    2.2.6.2   Milling
    2.2.6.3   Grinding
    2.2.6.4   Electrochemical
    2.2.6.5   Chemical
    2.2.6.6   Gears and bearings
2.2.7   Forming
    2.2.7.1   Cold-working processes
    2.2.7.2   Hot-working processes
2.2.8   Powdered metal processes
2.2.9   Heat treatment
2.2.10 Surface finishing and corrosion protection
    2.2.10.1   Shot peening and grit blasting
    2.2.10.2   Painting
    2.2.10.3   Plating
    2.2.10.4   Chemical conversion coatings
2.2.11 Adhesive joining
2.3   Nonmetals and composite materials processing
    2.3.1   Basic materials processing and process control
    2.3.2   Nonmetals and composites fabrication
    2.3.3   Adhesive joining
2.4   Dimensional metrology
    2.4.1   Fundamental units and standards
    2.4.2   Gaging
    2.4.3   Interferometry

Training References
Basic Materials, Fabrication and Product Technology

Materials & Processes for NDT Technology. Columbus, OH: The American Society for Nondestructive Testing, Inc. 1981.*

Taylor, J.L., ed. *Basic Metallurgy for Nondestructive Testing*, revised edition. Essex, England: W.H. Houldershaw, Ltd. (British Institute of Nondestructive Testing). 1988.*.*

Welding Inspection Handbook, third edition. Miami, FL: American Welding Society. 2000.

*   Available from The American Society for Nondestructive Testing, Inc., Columbus, OH.

PdM Basic Examination Level III Topical Outline

The PdM Basic examination will cover three main topical areas:

1.0   Personnel Qualification and Certification Programs
    1.1   *Recommended Practice No. SNT-TC-1A*
    1.2   *ANSI/ASNT CP-189*
    1.3   ASNT Level III programs

2.0   General Familiarity with Other PdM Methods

3.0   General Knowledge of Machinery

The PdM Basic examination and one or more PdM Method examinations (either thermal/infrared testing or vibration analysis) must be taken and passed to qualify for an ASNT PdM Level III Certificate. The endorsements on the ASNT Certificate will list the various methods, which the applicant passed.

1.0 Personnel Qualification and Certification Programs
    1.1 *Recommended Practice No. SNT-TC-1A*
        1.1.1 Scope
        1.1.2 Definitions
        1.1.3 Nondestructive testing methods
        1.1.4 Levels of qualification
        1.1.5 Written practice
        1.1.6 Education, training and experience
        1.1.7 Training programs
        1.1.8 Examinations
        1.1.9 Certification
        1.1.10 Termination
    1.2 ASNT Standard *ANSI/ASNT CP-189*
        1.2.1 Scope
        1.2.2 Definitions
        1.2.3 Levels of qualification
        1.2.4 Qualification requirements
        1.2.5 Qualification and certification
        1.2.6 Examinations
        1.2.7 Expiration, suspension, revocation and reinstatement of employee's certification
        1.2.8 Employer recertification
        1.2.9 Records
        1.2.10 Referenced publications
    1.3 ASNT Level III Certification programs

2.0 Basics of Common PdM Methods
    2.1 Infrared testing
    2.2 Vibration analysis
    2.3 Oil/lube analysis
    2.4 Motor circuit analysis
    2.5 Alignment
    2.6 Thermal testing
    2.7 System performance

3.0 Machinery Technology
    3.1 Machine design
        3.1.1 Lube systems
    3.2 Electrical components
    3.3 Maintenance concerns
        3.3.1 Millwright concerns
    3.4 Machine components
    3.5 Engineering mechanics

Appendix A: Radiographic Safety Operations and Emergency Instructions Course

Note: This outline provides radiation safety subject matter that applies to multiple types of penetrating radiation. Instructors should consider the applicable type of radiation source and delivery system to be covered and tailor their use of these subjects accordingly.

1.0　Personnel Safety and Radiation Protection
　　1.1　Hazards of excessive exposure
　　　　1.1.1　General: alpha-, beta-, gamma-, neutron and X-radiation
　　　　　　1.1.1.1　Alpha particles
　　　　　　1.1.1.2　Beta particles
　　　　　　1.1.1.3　X-radiation
　　　　　　1.1.1.4　Gamma radiation
　　　　1.1.2　Specific neutron hazards
　　　　　　1.1.2.1　Relative biological effectiveness
　　　　　　1.1.2.2　Neutron activation
　　1.2　Methods of controlling radiation dose
　　　　1.2.1　Time
　　　　1.2.2　Distance
　　　　1.2.3　Shielding
　　　　　　1.2.3.1　Half-value layers
　　　　　　1.2.3.2　Tenth-value layers
　　　　1.2.4　Exposure shields and/or exposure rooms
　　　　　　1.2.4.1　Operation
　　　　　　1.2.4.2　Alarms
　　1.3　Personnel monitoring
　　　　1.3.1　Difference between dose and dose rate
　　　　　　1.3.1.1　Coulomb per kilogram (C/kg)
　　　　　　1.3.1.2　Gray (Gy)
　　　　　　1.3.1.3　Sievert (Sv)
　　　　1.3.2　Wearing of monitoring badges
　　　　　　1.3.2.1　Pocket dosimeters
　　　　　　　　1.3.2.1.1　Neutron monitoring dosimeters
　　　　　　　　1.3.2.1.2　Gamma- and X-ray dosimeters
　　　　　　1.3.2.2　Film badges
　　　　　　1.3.2.3　Thermoluminescent detectors (TLDs)
　　　　1.3.3　Reading of pocket dosimeters
　　　　1.3.4　Recording of daily dosimeter readings
　　　　1.3.5　"Off-scale" dosimeter – required activity
　　　　1.3.6　Permissible exposure limits
　　　　1.3.7　As low as reasonably achievable (ALARA) concept

2.0　Radiation Survey Instruments
　　2.1　Types of radiation instruments
　　　　2.1.1　Geiger-müller tube
　　　　2.1.2　Ionization chambers
　　　　2.1.3　Scintillation chambers, counters
　　2.2　Neutron radiation survey equipment
　　2.3　Reading and interpreting meter indications
　　2.4　Calibration frequency
　　2.5　Calibration expiration – action to be taken
　　2.6　Battery check – importance

3.0　Radiation-Area Surveys
　　3.1　Type and quantity of radiation
　　3.2　Establishment of restricted areas
　　3.3　Posting and surveillance of restricted areas

12.0 State and Federal Regulations

    12.1 Nuclear Regulatory Commission (NRC) and Agreement States – authority

    12.2 License reciprocity

    12.3* Radioactive materials license requirements for industrial radiography

    12.4 Occupational Safety and Health Administration (OSHA)

    12.5 Qualification requirements for radiography personnel

    12.6 Regulations for the control of radiation (state or NRC as applicable)

    12.7* Department of Transportation regulations for radiographic source shipment

    12.8 Regulatory requirements for X-ray machines (state and federal as applicable)

*   Topics may be deleted if the radiography is limited to X-ray exposure devices.

**   Required only by those personnel who will be involved in neutron radiography of explosive devices.

References

ASNT Study Guide: Industrial Radiography Radiation Safety. Columbus, OH: The American Society for Nondestructive Testing, Inc. 2009.*

Bossi, R.H., F.A. Iddings and G.C. Wheeler, tech. eds. and P.O. Moore, ed. *Nondestructive Testing Handbook*, third edition: Volume 4, *Radiographic Testing*. Columbus, OH: The American Society for Nondestructive Testing, Inc. 2002.*

McGuire, S.A., and C.A. Peabody. *Working Safely in Radiography*. Columbus, OH: The American Society for Nondestructive Testing, Inc. 2004.*

Staton, Jean. *Radiographic Testing Classroom Training Book* (PTP Series). Columbus, OH: The American Society for Nondestructive Testing, Inc. 2005.*

Bush, J. *Gamma Radiation Safety Study Guide*, second edition. Columbus, OH: The American Society for Nondestructive Testing, Inc. 2001.*

Code of Federal Regulations, Title 10, *Energy*, Part 34, *Licenses for Industrial Radiography and Radiation Safety Requirements for Industrial Radiographic Operations*, Sub-Part 43, *Training*. Available online at http://www.access.gpo.gov/nara/cfr/cfr-table-search.html#page1.

Suggested State Regulations for Control of Radiation (SSRCR), Part E, *Radiation Safety Requirements for Industrial Radiographic Operations*, Sec. E.17, *Training*, 1999. Available online at http://www.crcpd.org/SSRCRs/e-1999.PDF.

*   Available from the American Society for Nondestructive Testing, Inc., Columbus, OH.